LIVING
with
KILLER
BEES

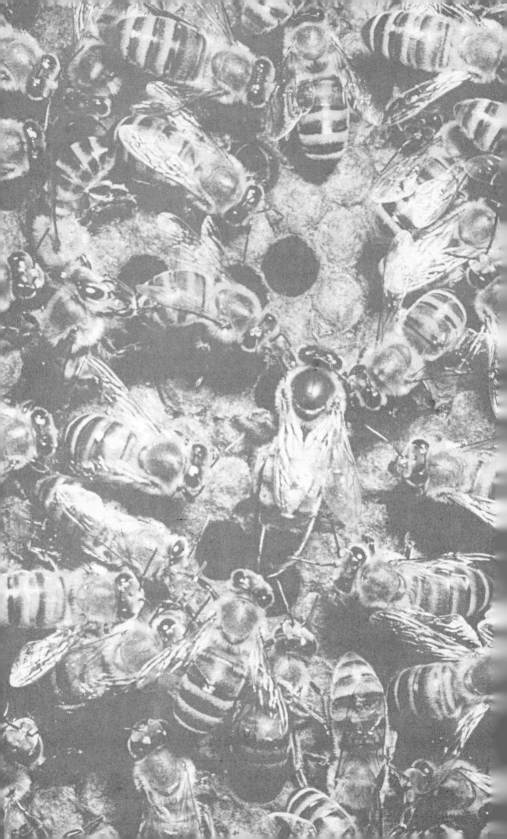

LIVING
with
KILLER BEES

The Story of the
Africanized Bee
Invasion

GREG FLAKUS

QUICK TRADING COMPANY
Oakland, California

First edition, November 1993

Technical Editing:
Kim Flottum
Hachiro Shimanuki

Cover photograph of Africanized Honey Bees in Brazil:
Norman Gary, Dept. of Entomology, University of California at Davis

Printed in the United States of America

Distributed by: Quick Trading Company
P.O. Box 429477
San Francisco, CA 94142-9477
(510) 533-0605

Publishers Group West

Publisher's Cataloging-in-Publication

Flakus, Greg.
Living with killer bees: the story of the Africanized bee invasion/Greg Flakus.
p. cm.
Includes bibliographical references and index.
ISBN 0-932551-12-2

1. Africanized honeybee. I. Title.

QL568.A6F53 1993 595.79'9
QBI93-1258

To Christopher,
the little guy whose love of nature inspired this book
and gave it purpose.

Contents

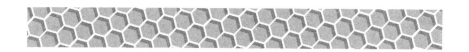

This is a book about a new arrival among living creatures in the United States — the Africanized bee, a particularly defensive and often dangerous breed of one of nature's most fascinating creatures — the honey bee. This book also concentrates on the human reaction to this insect phenomenon. Philosophers and poets going as far back as Aristotle have waxed eloquent about bees and the honey they produce. Getting stung has never been regarded as a pleasant experience, but even this has generally been portrayed as a minor, even comical occurrence and has done little to damage the image of the hardworking bee. However, the prospect of massive, perhaps even fatal, attacks by bees puts a different tinge on the subject.

The story of "killer bees," which are more properly called Africanized bees, may be viewed as a fascinating tale of species survival and proliferation; but it is also a cautionary tale about the consequences of tampering with nature. Nearly 40 years have passed since the first African queen bees were introduced to the wilds of Brazil, but there is still a great deal that is not known about the phenomenon. Experts from various Latin American governments and educational institutions have studied the African progeny, and entomologists and officials from the U.S. Department of Agriculture (USDA) have tracked the bees as they moved northward all the way to Texas. Yet even now, as they invade U.S. soil, experts argue over how far north they will ultimately go and how much of a threat they will pose to agriculture and to public safety.

My own experience with the Africanized bees has been mostly in Costa Rica, where I spent four years covering Latin American events for the Voice of America. My interest in the bees did not develop so much from my work as a journalist, however, as it did from my more dominant and demanding role as a father.

My wife, Aurora, and I are the parents of an inquisitive little nature boy named Christopher, who took full advantage of the exploration opportunities available at our home in Costa Rica's lush tropical highlands. Together, we kept vigil on two colonies of the stingless *Trigona* bees in our garden. These harmless creatures are native to Central America and Mexico and produce small amounts of honey. We also tracked leaf-cutter ants as they moved along highways they stomped with their little ant feet through our lawn and, with stomachs tightened, we observed the deft moves of a praying mantis eating worms off the leaves of a shrub. Through experience with Chris in our backyard jungle, I know full well how a child might innocently, or perhaps not so innocently, come in contact with bees. Children are naturally curious and this sometimes leads them into unpleasant encounters with nature. There have been many cases here in Latin America where children have disturbed hives of bees and have been attacked as a result.

My family and I lived just outside the Costa Rican capital of San Jose, in the mountainside village of Escazu. For some reason, wild bee colonies were constantly being discovered in the ravines and empty lots all around this area. In Costa Rica, any wild, unmanaged colony of honey bees is sure to be Africanized, what the local people call *"las abejas malas,"* the "bad bees" or *"las abejas asesinas,"* the "killer bees."

One afternoon in 1990, the entire main plaza of Escazu was emptied of people by a huge swarm of "bad" bees. By the time firemen and Red Cross workers got things under control and destroyed the colony, several people had been badly stung and required hospitalization.

In another incident, in July of 1991, a man who had decided to end it all took a taxi from another part of town and came to a ravine near Escazu that has often been favored by those who like the idea of leaping into the great beyond. The poor man bungled his jump and ended up on a ridge, where rescue workers could only reach him by lowering themselves down with ropes. In doing so, they disturbed a colony of *"las malas"* and soon, rescue workers, reporters and curious onlookers were all fending off angry bees. About the only person on the scene that day who avoided attack was the man who had tried to commit suicide. He was brought up and taken to a local hospital, where he remained morose, but unstung.

Examining the circumstances and details of such incidents gave me some insight into how and why the bees attack. I was also aided by Costa Rican beekeepers and researchers from the United States, who have made this Central American nation into something of a tropical laboratory for the study of many natural phenomena including Africanized bees. Officials in Mexico and Texas also provided me with information about the bees and about efforts aimed at minimizing their impact on apiculture, agriculture and the general public. I took information from these people and attempted to cast it in a form that would be more easily understood by the average person.

There is some disagreement among the experts who have studied these "bad" bees as to what they should be called. Some researchers believe the bees in the migrating front are purely African, in terms of their genetic attributes, and that they should be referred to as such, while others see a degree of hybridization with European bees in every population they examine. To avoid confusion, most experts have chosen to refer to the bees in Africa as "African" and their progeny in the Americas as "Africanized," and that is the approach taken in this book.

In the coming years, farmers, gardeners, hunters, hikers and other outdoor people, at least in the southern United States, will need to know about these bees in order to protect themselves. Hopefully, this book will help. Parents of small children, who live in areas where the bees have arrived, or are expected to arrive soon, may use this book as a way of educating their children on safety procedures, which are outlined in the final chapter. The best safety precaution, I believe, is knowledge. Once you understand the bees and their behavior, you are in a better position to avoid them and you are also in a better position to handle any possible encounter with them.

Hopefully this book will also spark some reader interest in bees, beekeeping, and insect life in general. In our increasingly urbanized society, we are so isolated from natural life that we have come to prefer it in the abstract. We may profess to love nature, but we don't want it scurrying around in our kitchen cabinets or biting our flesh as we try to sit in the shade in our own backyard. With our increased interest in ecology, however, should come the understanding that we are but one part of nature and that all living things have a place in this world we share. This includes insects and more to the point, it includes those creatures whom we may fear or dislike — mosquitoes, cockroaches, wasps, fire ants and — the subject of this book — "killer bees." Learning about something we regard as menacing can sometimes help us to put our fears into better perspective. The aim of this book is to do just that, while at the same time presenting some insights about nature and how we as humans can learn to cope with other natural beings.

A C K N O W L E D G M E N T S

Many thanks to all the people who gave me encouragement and advice in preparing this book, especially those who were consulted by mail, by phone, or in person to answer questions. If there is one person whose assistance and friendship was important from beginning to end, it was Ralph Iwamoto of the U.S. Agriculture Department's Animal and Plant Health Inspection Service (APHIS). His willingness to chat about his involvement with the Bee Regulated Zone in Mexico and the subject of bees in general kept me going on the right path. I also greatly appreciated the help of the following experts from USDA's Agricultural Research Service (ARS): Thomas Rinderer, Gerald Loper, Justin Schmidt, Anita Collins, Bill Rubink, Bill Wilson, Allen Sylvester, and Hachiro Shimanuki.

Others who were especially helpful and patient in answering questions from a non-expert were: David Roubik of the Smithsonian Tropical Research Institute in Panama; Orley Taylor of the University of Kansas; Roger Morse of Cornell University; Steve Taber, Villebrumier, France; Richard Adee, Bruce, South Dakota; Don Schmidt, Winner, South Dakota; Gene Killion, University of Illinois at Urbana-Champaign; Darrell Lister, Bellaire, Texas; and John Thomas, Fowden Maxwell, Dave Mayes and Kathleen Davis of Texas A & M University.

Much appreciation goes to Warwick Kerr of the Federal University of Uberlandia, Minas Gerais, Brazil for his correspondence.

In Mexico, *"miel gracias,"* as they say, to Salvador Cajero of the Agriculture Ministry's Africanized honey bee program, and Enrique Carrillo of Miel Carlota in Cuernavaca, Morelos.

In Costa Rica, I would like to thank Dr. William Ramirez, Dept. of Entomology, University of Costa Rica and beekeepers Nelger

Barrantes and Marcos Castro, who gave me some first hand experience in handling bees. I also wish to acknowledge the help, encouragement, and computer advice provided by fellow author Bill Baker.

Last, but certainly not least, I wish to express my appreciation to my wife, Aurora, and son, Chris, for their patience and support during the preparation of this project.

INTRODUCTION

by Hachiro Shimanuki
USDA/ARS Bee Research Laboratory
Beltsville, Maryland

"Living with Killer Bees: The Story of the Africanized Bee Invasion" is a historical account of the Africanized honey bee as it moves from Brazil to the United States. What makes this book different from its predecessors is that the author offers the readers an opportunity to delve into the thinking of scientists, beekeepers, and information specialists. Each of the interviewees offers different and sometimes controversial opinions on the past, present and future impact of the Africanized honey bees as they continue their seemingly unstoppable range expansion.

The honey bee is an essential part of our agriculture. When properly managed in the appropriate ecosystem, the honey bee is without doubt one of the most beneficial insects. Not only does it produce over 200 million pounds of honey annually, but over one million colony rentals are negotiated each year to pollinate some 100 cultivated crops valued in excess of $10 billion.

Unlike the problem of the parasitic mites which were essentially considered a beekeeper problem, the Africanized honey bee problem has a potential of affecting all phases of life in the United States. The Africanized honey bee will have an impact not only on how and where honey bees kept, but also on outdoor workplaces, school grounds, and recreational and residential areas. The magnitude of the problem will be determined in large part by public reaction. This book provides important information that many readers will find useful and goes far in assuaging fears of the Africanized honey bee.

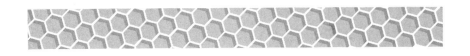

CHAPTER ONE

And now, live from south of the border...

The Latest
"Stinging Sensation"

INSECTS ARE NOT AMONG THE MOST POPULAR LIFE FORMS in the United States. Let's face it, people hate them! Extermination enterprises and manufacturers of insecticides and repellents have made millions of dollars seeking to protect us from the creeping, crawling and buzzing beasties that plague us. Entomologists, who devote their lives to studying insects, spend much of their time investigating new ways of protecting crops, animals and humans from the ravages of these un-loved little creatures. But, amongst themselves, in candid moments, the scientists who help develop the methods of attack against creepy critters often bemoan what they describe as America's "entomophobia." They see insects, spiders and various bugs as fascinating little beings who deserve more respect. Of course, animals get respect in direct proportion to the benefits they are seen as providing.

Of the tiny animals that share the planet with us, there are only a few that people generally accept as beneficial, even if they still regard them as disgusting or frightful. One is *Bombyx mori*, the silk moth, better known for the stage of development when it is a worm, producing the stuff that designers from Tokyo to Paris have put to good use. Butterflies are treasured for aesthetic reasons and because they do some pollinating. Ladybugs are cute and they are one of the

1

insects valued for their eating of other insects. But honey bees are, perhaps, the creatures with the best public image. We see them as industrious ("busy as a bee") and we appreciate their main product, honey, as setting the standard for all that is ecstatically wonderful and sweet. Health food enthusiasts see honey as an alternative to sugar and many home remedy proponents extol the use of honey as a cure for various ailments. We even call our loved ones "Honey" as a term of endearment. The Bible is full of positive references to honey, i.e. "the land of milk and honey." Prehistoric cave drawings show people harvesting honey from wild bee colonies and ancient Egyptian carvings depict early beekeeping activities. Sure, people got stung sometimes. Even Winnie the Pooh found that bees could get a little nasty when disturbed. But, in general, bees and their honey have a long, well-established history of acceptance and respect.

But while honey is nice, the honey bee's real importance lies in its excellent performance as a pollinator. The value of just the almonds produced in California each year with the help of honey bees is more than twice the value of all the honey produced in the United States in any given year. More than 100 agricultural crops in the United States are pollinated by bees and, although there are some bee species other than honey bees used for some of those crops, honey bees are the only ones that can be easily managed, moved around and used for a wide variety of crops. About 80 percent of the food Americans eat benefits from the pollination those little furry honey bees perform. Put in dollar terms, the crops pollinated by bees each year are worth about $10 billion. In addition, some vegetables are grown from bee-pollinated seed and, when you add to this the milk and meat from cattle and other animals which are fed from bee-pollinated crops, the above figure doubles. That means bees are important, if not essential, for the annual production of more than $20 billion worth of agricultural produce in the United States. (In addition, the honey bee contribution to pollinating vegetables grown in home gardens is valued at $1.4 billion a year!)

But now, all that is threatened by an invader — a foreign bee! It came to us from Africa, by way of Brazil, where it was introduced for genetic experiments almost 40 years ago. It migrated north and was first found in Texas in 1990. This is a bee that is said to attack for no good reason. This is a bee that is difficult to handle for beekeepers who want to move colonies around to pollinate various crops. This is a bee that often invades the colonies of "normal" bees and takes them over in a sort of insect blitzkrieg. This a bee that has been depicted in science fiction movies like "The Swarm" and "The Savage Bees" as threatening our lives, our property and our whole way of life. This bee is a "killer!"

There has been so much hype and so many jokes about "killer bees" that many people are justifiably confused about them. Are they a real threat or an exaggeration concocted by tabloid journalists and science fiction writers? Is their arrival a cause for alarm or should they be dismissed as a gag on the order of the late John Belushi's "killer bee" skits on Saturday Night Live in the 1970s?

Killer Bees, Saturday Night Live: (r to l) Gilda Radner, Chevy Chase, and John Belushi. Photo from The National Broadcasting Corp. Inc.

The simple answer is that they are neither a gigantic threat to public health and welfare in general nor are they something to be dismissed as a joke. In our highly-urbanized society it is reasonable to assume that the average person will never encounter a nest of aggressive bees but it is, nonetheless, quite possible that, in the coming years, people who work and play extensively outdoors, at least in the southern part of the United States, will come into contact with these creatures and that many of these people will get stung. If they are far from help and are unprepared, some of them could die.

There is always a threat from any stinging insect, including some species of ants, wasps, hornets, bumble bees and ordinary honey bees. Someone who is highly allergic to the venom of one of these insects could die from a single sting if not treated promptly. What makes the Africanized bee especially dangerous is its well-established tendency to attack furiously in large numbers. A normal person can withstand a few dozen stings without problem but hundreds of stings can prove fatal even to healthy adults.

Documented cases of stinging incidents in Latin America that have occurred over the past 30 years provide a disturbing picture of just how bad it can get. In Brazil, at least 200 people and countless numbers of animals have died from bee stings. Some of the first graphic accounts of "killer bee" attacks to reach the North American press came from Brazil. There were reports of whole towns under attack. There were gruesome stories of bees descending by the thousands on elderly people, children and the disabled — people who were unable to run away quickly and who were thus more vulnerable. But even healthy adults in seemingly benign situations felt the sting of the maddened bees. Firemen in one small town used flamethrowers to subdue a mass of bees that killed a local school teacher. In another well-publicized case, a man took a thousand stings to the head. The pain was so horrible that he got a gun and ended his own life. By 1976, even the bustling and vivacious city of

Rio de Janeiro was feeling the sting, as bees began attacking motorists on suburban roads. In one incident near Rio, a school bus with 50 high school students plunged off a bridge and crashed into a light pole where Africanized bees had built a nest. The angry bees soon created a worse problem than the crash itself. Firemen came to the rescue to fight off the bees and rescue workers took 46 people to a local hospital for treatment.

The Africanized bees reached Argentina by 1967 and by the mid '70s, they were kicking up a storm in that nation's northern, tropical regions. In 1975, they attacked 18 people in the town of El Carmen, near the Bolivian border, killing a six-year-old boy and seriously injuring two others. Reacting to the slightest provocation, the wild bees often seemed to go on a rampage. They struck a burial ceremony in one town, sending mourners running from the cemetery in panic. They attacked pedestrians and passengers in vehicles on a major highway bridge, injuring several people and causing police to close off the bridge until the bees could be destroyed. In an attack that rivaled anything Hollywood could have cooked up, the angry bees went into the control tower of the airport in the northeastern city of Salta, attacking Ricardo Mamani as he was trying to direct air traffic. Airport employees rescued him and firemen killed the bees with a blast of water.

In Venezuela, the Africanized bees really earned their reputation as *abejas asesinas*, "killer bees." The bees claimed some 400 lives within the first several years after they entered the country in 1976. They also caused consternation among the neighbors of backyard beekeepers. Often, when people or animals came under attack, mobs took their fury out on the nearest beekeeper, destroying the hives and burning the beekeeper's equipment and facilities. In many cases, the mobs destroyed relatively docile European bees in the bee yards in retaliation for the attacks committed by wild colonies of the fast-invading Africanized bees. Many of Venezuela's beekeepers were poor, rural people who had kept a colony or two in the backyard, along with the chickens and pigs. They soon lost their animals to the stinging swarms and many ended up burning their own hives. Virtually all the backyard and hobbyist beekeepers in Venezuela eventually gave up because they were unable to cope with the African invasion.

In Costa Rica, around a dozen people have died as the result of attacks by the *abejas asesinas*, since the aggressive little buggers first crossed over from Panama in 1983. In one horrible incident, bees attacked an elderly man and his son. The old man was quickly overcome and his son was forced to run to his brother's nearby house with the bees in hot pursuit. The terrified family in the house, however, closed the windows and locked the door, leaving the man to die on the front porch. The fury of the newly-arrived bees baffled nature-loving Costa Ricans who had never seen such bizarre behavior from insects. In one case, two men in a rural field came under attack. One dove into some bushes and the other, who was mounted on a horse, made a run for it. The bees followed the rider and killed him. The man in the bushes survived.

One of the most internationally-publicized incidents occurred in July of 1986, in Costa Rica's northwestern province of Guanacaste. A group of university students and professors who had come to work on various natural science projects supported by the Organization for Tropical Studies was exploring some rock formations when one student suddenly started screaming. Inn Siang Ooi, a 20-year-old Malaysian biology student from the University of Miami had accidentally disturbed a colony of Africanized bees near the top of one rock outcropping. He was soon covered with furiously stinging bees. Other students, looking at him from some distance below, saw a dark cloud of bees covering his head. The more he swung at them, the more maddened they became. After failing in a desperate attempt to fight off the attack, Ooi fell down unconscious and became wedged in a crevice, with the bees still swarming over him.

At this point, Claudette Mo, a Brazilian veterinarian from the

University of Wisconsin, decided that someone had to do some-thing. They were in a remote rural area with no access to any form of emergency assistance. No one else in the group had any medical training, so Mo volunteered to make the rescue attempt. She also had the advantage of never having been stung by a bee before. Allergic reactions to bee stings come only after a person has been stung at least once, since the body has had no exposure to the venom and cannot, therefore, have developed an allergic response. Mo took along an adrenaline injector and covered herself the best she could with some mosquito netting. As she made her way up the rock formation, the bees began strafing her. The closer she got to the victim, the more bees came after her. Soon they were under the netting and coming into her face. They went up her nose and into her eyes. She stifled her growing sense of panic as long as she could but it was clear that, under the circumstances, she would not be able to reach Ooi and that she was now in danger herself. She had no choice but to retreat. The other students came to Claudette's aid and injected her with the adrenaline.

The furious bees would not allow anyone near Ooi's now lifeless body until sunset, several hours after the initial attack. It was later determined that he had been stung more than eight thousand times. Claudette Mo was taken to a hospital, where doctors removed more than 100 stings from her body. Her face had become swollen and she had developed nausea, possibly as a reaction to the adrenaline shot, but she recovered after a day or two of rest.

Since that time, Africanized bees have continued their spread and have attacked hundreds more people all through Central America and on into Mexico. By October of 1990, they had moved over the border into the United States and, in May of 1991, Jesus Diaz became the first person to be attacked by the invading bees on U.S. soil. He was mowing a lawn at a trailer court in the border city of Brownsville, Texas when bees, apparently disturbed by the smell of gasoline and the vibration of the motor, began coming after him. When they started stinging his head and shoulders, he leapt from his rider-mower and ran, perhaps literally, for his life. Diaz suffered only 18 stings and was treated at a local hospital. Authorities found the guilty colony, destroyed the bees and sent some of the little bee bodies to the USDA Bee Research Laboratory in Beltsville, Maryland, where entomologists, using a number of tests, confirmed them as Africanized.

In the coming year, there would be other stinging incidents in Texas. Some would involve ordinary bees, but, increasingly, investigators would find indications of African genetic influence in their bee autopsies. In 1992, helped by an unusually wet spring, the Africanized honey bees moved even farther northward into Texas. By late June, Texas officials were getting an average of one report of a stinging incident per day. Many of the cases were serious enough to require hospitalization. In June, a swarm was located and destroyed underneath a parked helicopter at an Air Force base outside of San Antonio and officials stepped up programs aimed at protecting urban and suburban areas from wild colonies. San Antonio and Corpus Christi had become the first cities in the United States to experience the threat of the Africanized bees, but by the end of 1992, they had made their way close to Houston and the state capital of Austin and were still migrating westward along the Rio Grande. The little buzzing demons were on the move and the Lone Star state had become their playground. On July 15, 1993, 82-year-old Lino Lopez became the first person to die from an Africanized honey bee attack on U.S. soil. He was stung 40 times after he tried to remove a swarm of bees from a wall in an abandoned building on his ranch near Harlingen, Texas. A pathologist who examined the victim's body said the cause of death was the pooling of fluid in the lungs in reaction to the sudden influx of bee venom. Samples of bees from the swarm that attacked Lopez were confirmed as Africanized both by Texas experts and by the USDA in Maryland.

At the same time, Mexican experts were finding Africanized swarms in such desert states as Sonora and Chihuahua, indicating that the bees were no longer just moving up the relatively wet, lowland coastlines but were also moving inland. They were hopping from one irrigated agricultural zone to another and closing in fast on the borders of New Mexico, Arizona and California. People in those states began calling their county agricultural extension offices with worried questions. Police and fire departments got calls from people who had seen bees and thought they might be the dreaded "killer bees." A few swarms were discovered near the Mexican border in July of 1993 and the death of a dog in Tucson was attributed to a colony that officials believed had "hitchhiked" up from the border area on a vehicle. Some officials found this premature over-reaction amusing, but others worried about how they would cope when the bees finally did arrive in large numbers.

In all the border states, authorities worked with beekeepers and bee researchers to develop management plans to deal with the problem. Turning to the experts has been helpful, but only up to a point, since they disagree on the extent of the threat and they also disagree on such critical points as just how far north the Africanized bees will go and to what extent their undesirable behavior can be altered through hybridization. The experts who downplay the threat from Africanized honey bees say the impact on public health in the United States will be almost insignificant statistically. While they acknowledge that the influx of Africanized bees probably will increase the number of insect-related deaths in the United States each year, they see this as a minor concern when compared to yearly deaths from automobile accidents, cancer, AIDS, murder or even accidental household poisoning. They note, correctly, that there are already around 40 people killed in the United States each year by various types of insect stings and that the increased threat caused by Africanized bees will hardly cause a hiccup on the statistical picture. They may be right, but it is doubtful that the families of individual victims in the United States will find the broad statistical picture all that comforting.

Africanized bee on the left, European bee on the right — can you see any difference?
Photo courtesy Agricultural Research Service, USDA

Besides, our greatest fears are not always rational, and the demons that haunt our nightmares are often things from the natural world that have been exaggerated in our subconscious mind. Justin Schmidt, an expert on stinging insects and their venoms, has suggested that fear of insects in general may originate in the early experiences of humankind in the wild: "Modern man with his vehicles and other conveniences, and with his rich diet and long life span is only a very recent development in the long human history. During most of the evolution and history of humans, life spans were short and deaths were frequent due to diseases and other causes in nature. Death due to large predatory animals and to venomous animals was a real part of life. Under these conditions, our species would naturally develop a fear of animals, including stinging insects, that directly attack our bodies."

Schmidt says people often seem oblivious to statistical evidence about real dangers. They risk developing cancer or heart disease by continuing to smoke, drink alcohol and eat fatty foods, for example, because these activities have only an indirect relation to death and, since our primitive ancestors had no experience with these dangers, we have no basic, primordial fear of them. Meantime, the fear of being overwhelmed by a mass of stinging insects, "killer bees," for example, sends a chill right down the old spine.

The key to sorting out irrational fears from reasonable concerns is knowledge. To understand the threat of Africanized honey bees, it is necessary to know something in general about honey bees and their behavior. Even the seemingly bizarre attacks of the Africanized bees described above make sense once we understand their survival instincts and how they developed. Honey bees, whether they are European or African, do not go out of their way to sting us. In fact, as is explained in the next chapter, individual bees have more to lose in the encounter than we do. Bees of any type are neither bad nor benign. They have their own needs and their own highly-organized system of providing for the survival of their species. Understanding their system and their behavior is the first step in avoiding the nasty consequences of interference with their world.

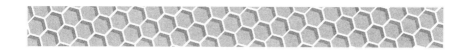

CHAPTER TWO

Bee Basics

THERE ARE AROUND 20 THOUSAND SPECIES OF BEES IN THE world, at least six of which are called honey bees. There are some solitary bees, but the more highly-developed bees are social creatures like the bumble bee and the honey bee. The bumble bees are the big, fuzzy looking guys you most often see in your garden. Honey bees are smaller and much more prolific. Not all bees sting but that does not make them innocuous. Some tropical stingless bees found in Central America can inflict painful bites.

Wasps and hornets, cousins of the bees, are capable of stinging and they will also defend their hives when disturbed. Yellowjackets, in particular, sting a lot and are often mistaken for bees. If disturbed, even a single wasp can provide nasty, multiple stings with its smooth lance. Wasps will sometimes try to set up their hives on the side of a house or under the portion of the roof that extends out from the house. Their nests can reach the size of a basketball and are made of mud combined with paper the wasps produce themselves. Wasps were making paper long before any human got the urge to write a letter, but there is nothing in a wasp's nest you would want to eat.

Honey, I'm home!

Honey bee nests are usually not exposed to the elements. The bees generally prefer enclosed areas, but sometimes do construct hives in trees. These will often feature several drooping combs full of amber-colored honey. Honey bees construct hives to store food and to raise more bees. The six-sided, white wax chambers that make up the honeycomb inside the hive vary in size according to the purpose. Some cells are for pollen and others for honey. Smaller chambers are for raising female worker bees; larger ones are for raising male drones. Queen chambers are also larger and longer. The comb is made of beeswax, a substance secreted from worker bee abdominal glands. Other construction in and around the hive is done with propolis, a sticky substance bees gather from trees and plants.

Of course, the most important product found in the hive is honey, but there are other riches as well. Worker bees who take on the role of nurses also produce a substance called royal jelly from special glands in their heads. This is given to the larvae that are to develop into queens and is also prized by many health food consumers for its nutritional value. Pollen stored in the honeycomb is used as a source of protein in feeding all the developing larvae, known as the brood.

Part of the reason honey bees are so important as pollinators is that they seek out flowers with pollen, unlike pollinators such as bats and hummingbirds, who are primarily interested in nectar. They also have lots of little hairs on their bodies. A furry little bee wiggling around inside the flower picks up a lot of pollen. But the thing that really makes honey bees the world's pollinators par excellence is that there are so many of them. Each full-sized hive, at the height of the growing season, contains an average of 40 thousand individual bees. Some well-managed hives in bee yards contain up to 80 thousand bees. These numbers can also make honey bees dangerous when aroused, since a disturbance can provoke an eruption from the hive of several thousand angry bees.

The honey bee is known to scientists as *Apis*, from which comes the word for beekeeping, apiculture, and the word for a bee yard, apiary. Of the six or more species of honey bee, the one commonly found today in Europe, Africa, the Middle East and the Americas is *Apis mellifera*, which means honey carrier, although technically the bees carry nectar from flowers which they then use to produce honey back in the hive. There are several subspecies of this highly-organized social insect, ranging from the relatively gentle and easy-to-manage Italian bee, *Apis mellifera ligustica*, which has long been favored by beekeepers, to the more aggressive German bees, *Apis mellifera mellifera*, who are larger and somewhat testier. Since they are all of the same species, bees from one subspecies can mate with bees from another subspecies, creating even more variation within the honey bee universe.

South of the Sahara

There are several honey bee subspecies found in Africa, including *Apis mellifera adansonii*, which inhabits the marsh lands of West Africa, and *Apis mellifera scutellata*, which is from eastern and southern Africa. This is the bee that started the whole phenomenon known as Africanization after it was introduced to South America nearly 40 years ago. (For a while, scientists were confused on the name and mistakenly referred to the imported bees as *Apis mellifera adansonii*, but there is agreement now that *scutellata* is the proper name for the progenitor of Africanization.)

An individual honey bee is no bigger than the top joint of your little finger and, being so small, would not get much respect in the animal kingdom, if it were not for its sting. Honey bees use this weapon to defend themselves and their colonies, but the reactions of various types of bees to perceived threats vary from mild and almost docile to angry and mean. The bees of the *scutellata* subspecies are in the latter extreme. They are far more defensive than any variety found in Europe. They are generally very quick to respond to any perceived threat and are also ten times more likely to attack in large numbers than bees from other areas. Entomologists believe these African bees developed their cranky attitude over thousands of years through the process of natural selection, just as the milder character of European bees was shaped by the environment.

European bees had to develop tactics for dealing with winter, storing sufficient honey for the cold months and also developing a means of keeping warm. They did this by learning to form a tight ball of bees around

European honey bees are much calmer than the Africanized variety, and can easily be marked for research studies. Photo courtesy Agricultural Research Service, USDA.

their queen to conserve heat. During the warm months, the European bees had wonderful foraging opportunities, abundant water, and relatively few predators. The European bees also had a regular, dependable change of seasons every year.

By contrast, the African bees had a year-round warm climate with frequent droughts and often unpredictable weather patterns. They also had to contend with a wide variety of predators who attacked and destroyed colonies that were anything less than fierce. Among the predators were human beings, who depicted themselves in rock drawings applying fire and smoke to hives to rob the bees of their sweet product. In Europe, there are similar prehistoric art works showing people stealing honey but not destroying the hives. Both bees had to develop some defensive capabilities, but the Africans may have had more compelling defense needs than the Europeans.

So, rather than view the African honey bees as a bunch of aggressive little bullies, they might be seen as tough little survivors who do not suffer any attempts against their security without providing a quick, effective response. What this means in practical terms is that African bees set up a perimeter equal in some cases to two or three city blocks in size and, depending on the time of year and other factors, react defensively to any perceived threat in that area.

Life in the hive

In most respects, the African honey bees live and act just as the European honey bees do. They both build a nest that develops into an organic unit (colony), in which the survival of the whole is supreme and individuals are frequently sacrificed to this end. This creation of a complex, unified community from thousands of individual beings is one of the things about honey bees that has fascinated people throughout the ages. Ants and termites also do this, but they are more often regarded as pests, and besides, they don't make honey.

The vast majority of honey bees in any hive are female worker bees, who perform such tasks as foraging, housekeeping and guarding the hive entrance. The male members of the colony, the drones, are somewhat larger and make up only about five percent of the hive population. The drones are the couch potatoes of the insect world. They hang around the hive and chew on honey and for the most part just get in the way of the workers. Occasionally they fly out to test their wings but their only real purpose is to participate in one race-to-death flight in which they attempt to pass their sperm to a queen. European bees generally kick their drones out as winter approaches and the colony must hunker down and conserve resources. The workers just push the lazy drones out of the hive and let them starve.

There is one female queen bee to every colony and her main job is to keep little bees coming. For this reason, she takes what is known as a "nuptial flight" sometime within the first week or two after she has emerged from her chamber. That is when the drones get their chance to make bee whoopee, as it were. The queen generally will mate with five to eight separate drones before calling it a flight and heading back to the hive. Some queens mate with up to 17 drones before calling it quits.

Honey bees engage in what might be called "killer sex." Instead of making love in the warm hive or amid the flowers, they perform their coupling during a high speed chase, flying up to 100 feet in the air. Inside the hive, the drones and queen don't pay much attention to each other, and indeed, there is no reason for them to do so, since queens do not mate with drones from their own hive. But once a queen flies out of the hive to an area where drones from other hives congregate, an aerial space that has been dubbed "the drone zone" or "drone congregating area," the queen signals her intentions by releasing a chemical signal, called a pheromone, that has most perfumes used by human females beat cold in terms of its effect. The drones love this stuff, and once they get a whiff of it, they go after the queen like fighter planes scrambling for action.

Only a few of the pursuing drones make contact with the queen and when they do, they go out in a blaze of ecstasy. The drones lose their seed, their genitalia and their lives in the process of mating. The "pop" sound made by their sex organs tearing off can actually be heard from the ground. Whether they have a good time doing this is hard to say since the poor little buggers die in the process. There is no bragging back at the drone locker room.

Once the queen has had her fill — and that is meant quite literally since she takes in as many as five million sperm in a flight — she heads back home to start laying eggs in beeswax chambers that the workers have created especially for this purpose. A queen can lay her own weight in eggs every day and, since she can maintain the sperm she has collected for her lifetime in a special pouch in her body, she can continue laying eggs indefinitely. The old expression "busy as a bee" has real merit when applied to a pregnant queen. The fertilized eggs laid by a queen produce female worker bees and new queens, but the queen also lays some unfertilized eggs, which produce the drones. (Many nonvertebrate animals are capable of asexual reproduction. In the case of honey bees, the eggs laid by the queen are parthenogenetic, which means they develop whether fertilized or not.) Since they come from unfertilized eggs, the drones carry only the chromosomes of the queen.

Queen bees live for about three years, on average, although some have been known to keep going for up to six years. While she is alive and pumping out eggs, the queens are constantly cared for by workers acting as attendants. In cases where a queen dies prematurely and the colony has no new queen to replace her, some worker bees develop the ability to lay eggs but, because they cannot mate, they produce only drones and the colony eventually perishes.

Activity in the hive looks something like the Los Angeles freeway system seen from above, except that there are no lanes. The bees just crawl all around and over each other, each going about her separate task. Communication is accomplished through a dance language, in which the scout bees maneuver and waggle. This is mainly used to inform everyone about the existence of, as well as the location of, a great foraging opportunity. When honey bees go in search of a new nesting site, scout bees go out to find a suitable location and then return to do a flying version of the dance, which tells the other bees what has been found and where it is. There can be more than one scout returning with such a pitch and somehow the mass of bees chooses one to follow. This is as close as bees get to politics.

Honey bees also use chemicals to communicate; the pheromone used by the queen in mating being just one example. Pheromones are also used to identify each other, to nest, and to defend. The queen maintains behavioral control of the colony by producing a pheromone known as "queen substance." As long as that stuff is being passed around, the message in the colony is that "we have a queen and all is well." When bees sting, they release an alarm pheromone to alert others to the danger.

Bees are sensitive to other smells as well, and for this reason people who wear colognes and perfumes outdoors often find themselves under close scrutiny, or even attack by the buzzing creatures. Beekeepers say the insects are also sensitive to foul odors and are particularly intolerant of uncleanliness. A person who has not bathed for some time might find him/herself the target of attack in a bee yard, while other people are left relatively unmolested. Honey bees are attracted to sweets, especially liquid sweets in the form of open bottles of soft drinks. This is why they sometimes gather around eating areas at open air events, like fairs and carnivals, and crawl around on the straws and bottle tops. While bees are generally not very aggressive while foraging, they can sting when disturbed, which makes them quite unwelcome at such events. Another problem can develop when wild bees establish their colonies in roofs, walls and attics, where they leave sweet-smelling residues that linger even after they abandon their home. These residues can attract other bees, who then make their nest in the same place.

The African traits

Other than their super defensive tendency, the African bees have only a few other characteristics that differ from ordinary, European honey bees. They are slightly darker and smaller; even the cells the Africanized bees build in the honeycomb measure smaller than those of European bees. There are also some slight differences in certain body parts, such as the veins in the wings, which can be measured. These characteristics, however, cannot be distinguished easily with the naked eye. Even an expert looking at a European bee and an Africanized bee sitting on the same leaf could have trouble telling which is which. Researchers have developed measurement tests that can be used in the field for a preliminary identification but more extensive tests are generally required for a positive identification.

One possible reason for the success of Africanized bees in displacing milder-tempered bees is that in every respect, the Africans appear to be more efficient and more diligent. They get up earlier, work later and visit more flowers per foraging flight than do European bees. When the moon is bright, Africanized bees will often continue to forage late into the night. This workaholic attitude even extends to reproduction. Africanized queen bees lay eggs at a slightly faster rate than do their European counterparts. Colonies of African and Africanized bees also produce a significantly larger number of drones than do those of European bees.

The Africanized bees are nervous in behavior. They tend to swarm more often and they are also more likely to abscond. "Swarming" occurs when part of the colony breaks off with the queen and flies off looking for another place to call home. The bees engorge themselves on their honey reserves before leaving so as to have sufficient energy to make it to a new location. There can be multiple swarms from one hive, since new queens can also emerge and fly off with part of the colony. When bees "abscond," they all take off to find a new nest. Bees typically abscond when they sense a threat to their colony or when they detect signs that foraging opportunities have almost been exhausted in the present location. Africanized bees are more sensitive to threats than are other bees and they have also been selected over centuries to survive in areas where scarcity of resources is common and absconding is the only alternative if the colony is to survive. The tendency of Africanized bees to leave home at a moment's notice makes them more difficult to manage and can limit the amount of honey that can be harvested from their hives.

Swarming is a term used by the general public to describe any congregation of flying insects, but beekeepers use it as a technical term, referring to breakaway colonies, as described above. To the

Honeybee serenade — only experienced beekeepers should try this!
Photo by Patrick O'Donnell

average person, a swarm of bees may look dangerous. But bees are not predatory, they do not attack without provocation and, if anything, bees in swarms are more docile than normal because they have no home to defend. They are usually incapable of stinging, since their little bellies are so full of honey that they literally cannot bend their abdominal area to insert the sting. Swarms often attach to tree branches in impressive, hanging conglomerations. Beekeepers seek out such swarms because they are easy to capture and place in a managed hive. You may have seen photographs of beekeepers scooping up bees by the handful or allowing the bees to swarm all over their bodies. They do this by applying pheromone or some honey first, so that the bees will be attracted to them. Another trick is to put a queen bee on your chin so that the swarming bees form a "bee beard." In order for these tricks to work, the bees have to have just eaten a good amount of honey or sugar water so that they are docile. But only an experienced beekeeper should approach a swarm in the wild. These tricks are NOT recommended for amateurs.

Honey, I love you!

The honey produced by African and Africanized bees is the same as honey produced by other bees. Eating the honey produced by the aggressive bees will not lead to aggressive behavior in humans. No doubt this will come as a disappointment to many of our trial lawyers who might have thought of using "killer bee" honey consumption as a defense for clients accused of murder and mayhem. (Recall the so-called "twinkie defense," in which lawyers tried to defend a client on the basis that he had been driven to crime by eating "junk food" and the "boob tube defense," in which a client was said to have been driven to lunacy by watching an excess of television.)

Bees produce honey and other products useful to humans as part of their natural mission to create a self-sustaining community. Honey is produced from nectar collected from flowers, combined with enzymes produced by the bees. The flower advertises itself to the bees with colorful petals, each of which contains streaks of ultraviolet color, invisible to the human eye, which, like airport runway lights, guide the bees to the nectar. The visiting bee then moves her head down into the flower to ingest some of the sweet liquid. In the process, as was mentioned above, she picks up pollen which is carried along to the next flower. The transfer of pollen, which basically consists of male reproductive cells, from the stamen of one flower to the female portion, or pistil, of another flower, is the method through which many plants accomplish fertilization. As for the bee, she takes her belly-full of nectar back to the hive and gives it to a "house bee," who mixes it with enzymes and then deposits it into a chamber where it remains exposed to air for a time to allow some of the water portion to evaporate. The bees help the process along by fanning the open chambers with their wings. The honey is later capped with beeswax and kept for future use.

Honey bees pick up pollen on all their body hairs, but move it to special hairs on their hind legs, that work like little baskets. Foraging bees returning to the hive often have little balls of pollen hanging from these hind leg hairs. They store the pollen in the hive as a protein-rich food for developing larvae. There is evidence that Africanized bees spend more time collecting pollen than do European bees, because, researchers say, they need extra protein to produce more brood. This is part of the African tendency to favor expansion and frequent division of the colony, as opposed to the European tendency to build up large, stable colonies full of honey for the winter.

During those hard times when there are few foraging opportunities, bees sometimes raid other, weaker colonies looking for honey to steal. The robber bees cannot saunter into a different hive unnoticed. Guard bees at the hive entrance usually try to fight off invaders in little sting duels. Africanized bees have a noticeable tendency to raid other colonies, especially during periods of drought or famine.

In regard to these inter-bee battles, it should be noted that a honey bee can sting another bee more than once, but if she stings you or your pet dog, you have the satisfaction of knowing she won't be stinging anyone again. As is the case of the poor drone having sex, the female worker bee usually sacrifices her life in stinging an animal or a human in defense of her hive. This occurs because the honey bee sting has a barbed end which gets caught in the skin. The bee literally tears her insides out trying to extract the sting after having sunk it into the victim's flesh. Queen bees also have stings and use them in battles with each other for dominance of the colony. If a new queen emerges from her incubation cell and is detected by the current queen, the "old lady" often goes over and knocks off her rival. In this way, the stability of the colony is maintained. When a queen gets old or weak and slows her production of queen substance, she is generally supplanted by a new queen.

The sting employed by bees evolved thousands of years ago from an ovipositor, a tube on the tail which was used for laying eggs. This change occurred in many, but not all, of the 70,000 species of the biological group *Hymenoptera*, which includes bees, wasps and ants. The sting is nature's way of giving these little animals an edge over much larger creatures. The venom generally contains small amounts of toxic material as well as chemicals to produce pain. Nature's strategy here is to inflict some immediate punishment to chase potential attackers away and to do more serious damage to those who do not run away fast enough.

For the most part, honey bees maintain their remarkably stable and organized colonies without much violence. Attacking is not the only defense mechanism at the bees' disposal. As was mentioned above, bees can also move away from threats. The Africanized honey bees, as will be discussed later, have spread through most of the Americas partly because of their tendency to favor frequent moves. Their biggest move, however, crossing the Atlantic from Africa to Brazil, was not done through their own initiative. There was a man who helped them on that one.

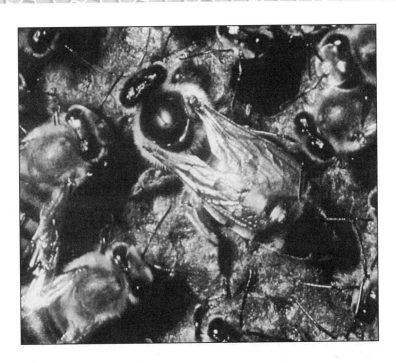

Beekeeping Basics

PEOPLE HAVE BEEN HARVESTING HONEY FOR THOUSANDS OF years, starting by simply taking the honey from wild bees, and getting stung in the process, but later developing methods of maintaining the bee colonies in devices they constructed for that purpose. Primitive hives included hollowed logs, holes built into mud walls, cones made of mud, earthenware, or thatch. These served the basic purpose of housing the colony, but were quite limited from a management standpoint. Still, beekeeping became an important activity in much of the ancient world. The Egyptians were keeping bees 2,500 years ago and the Greeks and Romans continued the practice.

Photo above: Queen on comb. She is larger than the workers and has a smooth thorax. Photo by Ralph Iwamoto

Bees are not domesticated animals, the way cows and chickens are. Bees are "kept" only in the sense that the beekeeper provides them with a place to establish themselves and then manages them so that he or she can collect the honey, beeswax, royal jelly, and pollen. The beekeeper must also continually monitor the colony to prevent anything from happening to the bees that might affect that harvest. Bees will swarm in the spring if they can produce new queens. Since beekeepers want large colonies to produce lots of honey, they usually try to prevent swarming by finding and removing queen cells. Once there is a queen larva growing, however, they must try to control the swarming process. Sometimes they do this by splitting the colony and providing a virgin queen to the queenless part. The beekeeper can also help prevent swarming by making sure the hive does not get too crowded or uncomfortable. In temperate climates, the beekeeper generally must feed sugar syrup and protein to the colony during the late spring, so that there will be a strong colony for the nectar flow season.

Modern beekeeping pretty much started in 1851 with the perfection of the moveable frame hive box by Lorenzo Langstroth, an Ohio minister and beekeeper. The basic principle involved is that of "bee space," which is the gap (¼ to ⅜ of inch) bees leave between the combs they build in the wild. The frames set in the hive box are kept that distance apart so that the bees will feel comfortable and build their comb on the frame, without adding any bridgework combs between frames. The frames can then be easily removed the way files are pulled up from a file cabinet.

A normal apiary hive is actually a series of stacked boxes. The brood chamber is on the bottom, with the boxes for honey storage, called supers, on top. Each super contains eight to ten frames. At harvest time, the honey is removed from the frames by first cutting the wax capping off the tops of the cells and then placing the whole frame in a cylindrical device, called an extractor, which is spun fast so that the honey is pulled out by centrifugal force. It is then filtered to remove any particles of comb or other impurities.

Beekeepers who manage European colonies often work with very little extra clothing. Sometimes a hat and veil are sufficient. When bees are testy, a full bee suit and gloves may be donned. When working with Africanized bees, however, it is often necessary to use a full suit made of white nylon or cotton material, on top of overalls or another bee suit. Thick plastic or leather gloves can also protect the hands. Even with these precautions, some beekeepers need to work the bees at night or use lots of smoke to calm them.

The smokers employed by beekeepers usually consist of a cylindrical device with a bellows attached. Slow-burning material is put in the cylinder and the beekeeper works the bellows to blow the smoke onto the hive box, the frames, or wherever it is needed. Smoke subdues bees and makes them settle on the comb where they slurp up all the honey they can get their little tongues into. This engorging makes them more docile and easier to handle. People working African bees have to use a lot of smoke. Often, two people have to work together, one doing the smoking and one opening the hive to perform whatever task is needed. In addition to their defensiveness, Africanized bees are also nervous and have a tendency to run off the frames, making it difficult for the beekeeper to find the queen when inspecting the colony. Although beekeepers in Africa and in many parts of Latin America have been successful in working the *scutellata* line, they find that it is often difficult and that special measures need to be taken.

CHAPTER THREE

The African Queens

AFRICANIZED BEES HAVE OFTEN BEEN PORTRAYED AS "foreign" invaders; unwelcome and uninvited. They have joined the ranks of such other notorious immigrant pests as fire ants, Asian cockroaches, Mediterranean fruit flies, the zebra mussels that are now clogging water and power plant intakes in the Great Lakes area, and the proliferating *Melaleuca* trees, an import from Australia that threatens to displace much of the natural vegetation in Florida. The judgment as to whether something imported belongs or not depends on its perceived effects.

The introduction of animal and plant species from one area of the earth to another has been an important part of history, and the effects have ranged from spectacularly successful to disastrous. Take rats, for example. The Norway rat, which destroys millions of dollars worth of food each year throughout the world, spreads disease, bites people and in countless other ways makes itself obnoxious, was spread to the far corners of the earth by shipping. Rats got on board sailing vessels, hid in the cargo and then scampered off at the various ports of call, seeking slimy new garbage heaps to roam. But in the cargo holds along with the rats were many plants and animals which humans were deliberately taking from one place to establish in another. The biggest transfer of species between regions of the world occurred in the first decades after the European discovery of the Americas. Europe got potatoes, tomatoes, corn, cacao, pineapples and turkeys. The American continents got horses, cows, sheep, chickens, wheat, coffee, bananas, oranges, and honey bees.

There were bees in the Americas before Christopher Columbus wandered on across the Atlantic in search of the Indies, and hundreds of varieties of these creatures still inhabit large areas of tropical America. The *Melipona* and *Trigona*, stingless bees found in Central America and parts of South America and Mexico, were used by native tribes in many areas as a source of honey. The ancient Maya civilization, which flourished in the Yucatan and in parts of Central America, had a fairly well-developed beekeeping industry. The Spanish bishop of Merida during the early colonial period, Diego de Landa, described the festivals of November and December, when the Mayas worshipped the god of honey, Ah-Muzencab, in the hopes of obtaining a good flow of nectar for their bees. The descendants of the Maya still work with these bees to some extent today in the Yucatan.

For more than two centuries after the Spanish and Portuguese arrived in the New World, the native stingless bees remained the primary source of honey in their colonies. However, these small bees produced very little of the sweet gooey stuff in comparison to Old World honey bees, so, in the early part of the 16th century, the Spanish began bringing over honey bee colonies to establish a bigger production capability. English colonists did the same and soon honey bees were escaping into the wild and buzzing all over North America. In some cases, honey bees in North America, travelling in advance of the European settlers, came in contact with western Indian tribes, who dubbed them "white man's flies." By the time the frontier had been settled, late in the 19th century, honey bees were regarded as a natural part of the natural world in North America.

By the twentieth century, many people in the tropical zones of South America had also developed a taste for honey and they imported more European bees to establish on their farms. But the South American beekeepers found that the production of the European honey bee was not entirely satisfactory and beekeeping remained a minor industry in all but a few places. The German, Spanish and Italian honey bees most commonly used never adapted well to hot, wet and humid conditions. The tropical American bee-keepers began thinking of how they might breed a bee better suited to their environment.

The Brazilian Connection

Some Brazilians thought the answer might be found in the tropi-cal zone of the continent located just across the Atlantic from Brazil: Africa. They had seen reports of beekeepers in South Africa getting remarkable production from native bees. Some African beekeepers had imported European bees but they had not done well. The Africans had more success with the indigenous bees of the sub-species *Apis mellifera scutellata*. African peoples had been obtaining honey from the wild bees for many centuries and, while they knew how furious the insects could get, they had also developed ways to avoid attack. In Africa's rural and wilderness areas, angry bees are among the lesser dangers humans can face. Beekeepers in South Africa, Angola, Mozambique, Kenya and Tanzania had been suc-cessful in working with the pure-bred Africans in managed colonies and they found them to be prolific honey-producers.

The Brazilians were particularly excited about reports they had read about South Africa's E.A. Schnetler and Angola's V. Portugal Araujo, who had produced prodigious amounts of honey using the native African stock. Schnetler had set records for honey production with his African bees, getting an annual average of about 150 pounds of the sweet stuff from each colony he maintained.

In 1956, the Brazilian Agriculture Ministry contacted Brazil's most prominent geneticist, Warwick Estevam Kerr, to see if he might be

Dr. Warwick Kerr, Brazil 1971.
Photo courtesy Norman Gary, Dept. of Entomology, UC Davis

able to obtain some African bee queens and bring them back for breeding experiments. Kerr had devoted himself to studying Brazil's native stingless bees and was therefore quite familiar with bee breeding and apiculture. In addition, he had just won his nation's top prize for genetics and was planning to spend the money that had come with it on a research trip to Africa.

Warwick Kerr thought there was a good possibility that he could utilize African stock to produce a new breed of bees, which would be less defensive than the wild African bees but which would be more productive than European bees in Brazil's tropical setting. After some initial difficulty in packaging bees for transport and keeping them alive, he returned to Brazil with 63 live queens he had obtained in South Africa from E.A. Schnetler and another bee-keeper, W. Crisp. These were later taken to a quarantine area at an agricultural research station near Rio Claro, in the state of Sao Paulo, where 48 were still alive and well as 1956 came to an end. By inter-breeding the queens through artificial insemination with European drones, Kerr and his associates had produced a number of first generation hybrids, which are known as F_1's in genetic terms (not to be confused with military aircraft). After several months of this activity, natural attrition reduced their stock of African queens to 29, and they were maintained in hive boxes equipped with queen exclud-ers. Remember that the queens and drones are larger than the worker bees who go out to forage. By putting a device over the hive entrance with holes too small to allow the queen to escape but large enough for the workers to pass, the normal activity of the hive was maintained while the danger of swarming was eliminated.

In October of 1957, however, according to the story that Warwick Kerr and his associates have told countless times, a local beekeeper wandered by, noticed the queen excluders and removed them. Such excluders are normally only used in the time before queens begin laying eggs and it is possible that the fellow was just trying to be helpful. In any case, as the story goes, the removal of the excluders allowed 26 African queens to escape with small swarms into the lush eucalyptus forest nearby. By the time Kerr learned of the accident, there was no way of figuring out where they had gone. He continued his work with the remaining African queens and hybrid queens thinking that perhaps the escaped bees would either perish in the wild or mate with European bees and eventually lose their African characteristics.

Within a few years, however, the researchers at Rio Claro began getting reports from surrounding rural areas of bees furiously attacking farm animals and even humans. Many poor Brazilian farmers suffered livestock losses and, eventually, there were human fatalities as well. By the early 1960s, it was clear that a rapid expansion had occurred among feral bee colonies and that the Africanized bees were moving quickly into other parts of the country. Whereas European swarms might go only a few miles and then look for an ideal place to establish themselves, the African progeny often moved 60 miles at a hop and built their nests in any hollow log or rocky ridge they could find. They worked fast and hard and produced more and more little bees, including new drones and queens, who quickly went out and bred with other bees, extending the feisty bloodline all through Brazil's honey bee population.

A Likely Story

While this escaped swarm story is generally accepted as the start of the Africanized bee problem in the Americas, there are many researchers who doubt this is the whole story. For one thing, Kerr and his associates never revealed the name of the man who supposedly removed the queen excluders. They said they wanted to protect him from publicity since he had not intended to create a disaster when he stuck his nose into their experimental apiary. The story is plausible and most people leave it at that, but a bigger question remains in regard to the feasibility of 26 queens in the wild producing the billions of Africanized bees that would eventually sweep across most of the western hemisphere.

David Roubik, a tropical bee specialist at the Smithsonian Institution's Tropical Research Institute in Panama, who has studied the Africanized bee phenomenon in various parts of Latin America, is among the skeptics.

"If there were only 26 colonies in the middle of the Amazon forest, nothing would have happened, ever," Roubik said in an interview conducted for this book. "They would never have successfully reproduced. I am afraid it is a bit of a fabrication. There may well have been those 26 colonies and all their drones and what have you, but there were other bees, too. They were hybrids, and there were not just 26 of them; there were thousands."

Roubik said he believes Warwick Kerr and his staff produced the hybrid queens, both before and after the alleged escape of the swarms took place, and distributed them to beekeepers far and wide, in an effort to build up the beekeeping industry, and to assist poor, rural Brazilians in the process. Roubik said he heard Kerr admit, in a 1984 speech in San Antonio, that the F_1 hybrids were the real problem. Kerr was speaking Portuguese, however, and Roubik, who also speaks Portuguese, believes most people in the audience, who heard only the English translation, did not understand the significance of what Kerr had said.

The story of the escaped queens being the origin of the Africanization problem also violates ecological principles, according to Roubik. "I am an ecologist in good standing," says Roubik, "and Allee's rule (minted in the 1920s) states than an introduced species brought in in such low numbers disperses and then can't find conspecifics with which to mate, and then completely dies out. This is what would have happened if there had not been F_1 hybrids — either from apiaries or from misguided efforts to circulate African-crossed-with-European F_1 queens — which still goes on in Brazil today!"

Other bee experts agree with Roubik that the rapid spread of

Africanization in the honey bee population of the Americas could only have occurred through a systematic introduction of thousands of hybrid queens to apiaries and, subsequently, through thousands of escaping swarms, to wilderness areas. They argue that the strong African traits would have been quickly diluted had only 26 swarms been involved and that, under normal conditions, natural predators and other factors would also have reduced the impact of the escaped bees.

Warwick Kerr has admitted that he did give hybrid queens to beekeepers in Brazil but he denies having carried out any widespread distribution. In a letter sent to the author, he says that between November of 1956 and October of 1957, when the escape took place, he distributed a total of 20 hybrid queens to local beekeepers and that, of those, only five survived. He also discounts the possibility that the hybrid queens would have produced break-away swarms that went into the wild to breed with the escaped queens since he believes the beekeepers were vigilant and were successful in preventing such swarms.

Kerr expresses some exasperation at colleagues from North America who question his story of the escaped queens as the beginning of the Africanized bee proliferation. "Many times I wonder why the Americans are eager for gossip," he complains. "It must be an excess of creativity!"

Roger Morse of Cornell University, who is considered to be one of the top experts on honey bees in the United States and who developed a friendship with Kerr while working for a time in Brazil, defends his South American colleague on this issue, calling the spread of genetic material from just 26 queens "a great lesson in biology."

However, a prominent Latin American bee expert who was consulted on this matter says that Kerr and his associates have been inconsistent in their descriptions of the escape over the years and that he believes they invented the story after it became apparent that the Africanized bees were creating problems for the general public.

The expert, who does not want his name used, said he discussed the story with Kerr himself once at a conference in Brazil and with a Brazilian beekeeper who had followed developments in the story from the start. He says what they told him left him with no doubt that the Africanization process had indeed started from the F_1 hybrids produced at the experimental apiary.

In Defense of Good Intentions

Most experts are reluctant to publicly air their disagreement with Kerr for two reasons. For one thing, he is an internationally-honored geneticist and he has put forth what many scientists accept as a plausible explanation of how the problem started. The other reason few people care to question his story is that most people who know him regard Kerr as a noble, courageous and generous man who has worked long and hard for the people of his country. One researcher who knows Kerr calls him "a saint."

Warwick Kerr stood out in Brazil not only for his scientific achievements, but because he was a Protestant in a Catholic land, and perhaps, because he was a man who had inherited a bit of a rebel's disposition. Kerr's grandfather, Warwick S. Kerr, was a Tennessee Confederate who moved his family to Brazil in 1864 after Union troops began occupying the South in the Civil War. He was one of about 10,000 North Americans to immigrate to Brazil around that time and, as a result, there are whole towns in Brazil today where Anglo surnames are common. Grandfather Kerr married twice in Brazil and produced 18 children. In November, 1992, the Kerr's had a reunion in Sao Paulo which drew 750 adult descendants of the old rebel. There are also more than 500 children under the age of 15 who will carry on the Kerr lineage.

Some of that contrarian rebel blood Warwick Kerr inherited from his grandfather may have played a role in the political problems he became involved in during the 1970s. At that time, Brazil was ruled by a repressive military regime, and Kerr was jailed twice after protesting the torture of political prisoners. Because of his international standing, the government released him both times after an overnight stay. He was told he ought to leave the country, but he refused. Roger Morse has gone so far as to say that much of the hysteria over "killer bees" was the result of Brazilian government propaganda designed to damage the image of Kerr internationally, as well as in his own country.

Kerr downplays his own heroism and says he doubts the repressive regime had anything to do with using the Africanized honey bee issue to attack him. He says he was jailed the first time in 1964, because he had complained about the torture of striking railroad workers. Kerr says the local, civilian sheriff won a bottle of beer in a barroom bet over whether he would have the courage to arrest the prominent scientist. Five years later, he was arrested again after he protested publicly against the brutal torture of Maurina Borges, a Catholic nun. Kerr says the sheriff was a bit puzzled by this prominent Protestant defending a Catholic nun and concluded that the bee researcher and the nun must have shared a common faith in communism. Kerr says the military commanders, upon hearing of his imprisonment, ordered his release because they knew that Brazil's communist party followed strict Russian rules, which he says meant, "no admission of geneticists or Christians was allowed."

The ugly atmosphere of repression persisted in Brazil until a more moderate regime came to power in February, 1974. A civilian, democratic government was restored in 1985. But before things got better, the pressure took a toll on Kerr. He suffered a nervous breakdown, partly because of the political situation and partly because of guilt over the people killed and injured by the Africanized bees he had introduced to Brazil.

Kerr says his guilt over the bees subsided somewhat in 1975, when the mayor of Crato, in the drought-plagued northeastern state of Ceara, visited him to thank him for having introduced the bees that were now saving hundreds of families from starvation. The poor people of this region had learned how to collect the honey and brood from Africanized bee colonies to provide nutritious, life-saving food for themselves and their children. In addition, Kerr was vindicated by the advance of beekeeping and honey production in Brazil. After initial setbacks, beekeepers learned to cope with the Africanized bees. Indeed, many of them came to prefer these bees because their super-defensiveness deters thieves.

Honey production in Brazil was insignificant before the arrival of the African queens; now Brazil is the second largest honey producer in Latin America and ranks fourth worldwide. David Roubik suggests that Kerr's original goal has been fulfilled. "Now they have bees that are adapted to beekeeping in the tropics that they never had before, and Warwick would say the same thing himself, that what they didn't count on was that it would have to be such a painful process to get to this point."

On this, Kerr more than agrees. In spite of the benefits Brazil has enjoyed from the introduction of the African bees, Kerr says none of it was worth the loss of life and the trauma suffered by many rural people who came under attack without warning. With hindsight, he says he never should have brought those African queens to Brazil. Instead, he says, he should have worked more with the native *Melipona* stingless bees to develop a larger Brazilian honey industry.

Today, Warwick Kerr, now in his 70s, continues his stingless bee studies at the University of Uberlandia, in the interior province of Minas Gerais. While many people will always remember him for his courageous opposition to political repression, his concern for the poor, and his pioneering work in bee genetics, it is his burden to also be remembered as the man who brought those nasty "killer" bees to the Americas.

CHAPTER FOUR

The Flight of the "Killer Bee"

THE TERM "KILLER BEE" IS DISDAINED BY MOST ENTOMOLOGISTS and absolutely detested by most beekeepers. Among USDA's bee bureaucrats, it is mentioned only as "the k-word." These people dislike the expression because of its science fiction associations and also because it is a somewhat misleading characterization of a creature that has many positive qualities from a biological point of view.

"Killer bees" is generally derided as "a media invention." But the term may, in fact, have come from a different source. Cornell University's bee expert, Roger Morse, as was mentioned in the last chapter, believes much of the hysteria over Africanized bees was deliberately manufactured by the military government that came to power in Brazil through a coup d'etat in April of 1964. According to Morse, the dictatorial goons invented the term "killer bees," (*albehas assassinas* in Portuguese), as part of their campaign to undermine Warwick Kerr's human rights activism. Morse says that many reports of bee attacks in that nation during the early 1960s were suspect. He says officials often counted any kind of insect stinging incident as a "killer bee" attack.

Eventually, the term "killer bees" found its way onto the pages of *Time* magazine's September 24, 1965 issue. Morse says the magazine was influenced by a Brazilian government press release. Kerr, on the other hand, says he does not recall hearing the expression used before it appeared in the *Time* article. In any case, it was the first use of the term in the North American media and from there it took on a life of its own.

Sue Hubbell, the author of some fine books about her beekeeping experiences in Missouri, suggested in an article published in the *Smithsonian* magazine of September, 1991, that the term "killer bee" should be scrapped and replaced with the term "bravo bee." This makes a nice word play, since bravo in Spanish can mean "fierce" and also has a positive implication as the word shouted from the audience after a particularly impressive performance at an opera or theater event. Indeed, Hubbell's point was that, for American beekeepers, the Africanized bee could be a great performer. The problem with her idea, however, is that beekeepers are a fairly small minority, whose perception of benefits from the bees will be of little interest to John Q. Public if he comes under attack while hiking through his favorite park. There is also some question as to just how well the Africanized bee will perform in the more temperate zones of North America and whether any amount of honey will be worth the cost of dealing with this difficult animal.

Journalists continue to use "killer bees" because the Africanized bees, after all, have killed a lot of people and animals, and the term is one that is familiar, is readily understood by the public, and has a certain whimsical appeal. The use of such shorthand is a well-established journalistic technique. Just one word — "Watergate" — provides reference to a whole complex series of events in a scandal that brought down a president. Pentagon briefers may not like the press use of "Star Wars," but how many people recognize the term "Strategic Defense Initiative?"

Scientists, too, sometimes complain about pedestrian translations of their complicated jargon, but they themselves have coined some of the better ones: "black hole" for a collapsed star, the "big bang" theory of how the universe got started and "buckyballs," a term derived from Buckminster Fuller which chemists use to label spherical frameworks of carbon atoms. Colorful slang of this sort can also be useful in drawing public attention to a problem scientists would like to investigate. Many an article by a bee expert makes passing reference to the term "killer bees," if only to dismiss it as inappropriate. In so doing, however, the writer connects with the central issue of concern to most people, which is the trouble and danger this insect may bring. Public fear of the "killer bees" has helped many a researcher locate grant money or government support. After all, entomologists would spend most of their time on esoteric subjects of little interest to the general public if it were not for the occasional appearance of an insect menace.

In the Research Trenches with Apis mellifera scutellata

After the first media reports of "killer bees" appeared in the United States, researchers from North America began swarming all over Brazil, and other nations that had been invaded by the Africanized bees, to make an assessment of the situation and to separate myth from fact. Sometimes, they found, the facts supported the myth. In 1972, a committee from the National Academy of Sciences issued a report that seemed to confirm many of the worst fears planted in the public mind by the news media.

The report said: "Because of its unprovoked mass stinging, and because of frequent swarming and absconding, the Brazilian bee is dangerous to people and animals and is difficult to manage." The committee went on to recommend that "every effort be made to prevent the Brazilian bee from reaching North America."

Some researchers started looking at possible control methods, while many others took a more "pure science" approach, investigating the spread of Africanized bees as a fascinating biological phenomenon, which it certainly was, and continues to be. Unfortunately, some of the work overlapped and duplicated work already done by Brazilian researchers. Portuguese, the language of Brazil, is not as widely-spoken as English, Spanish, or French and research papers from Brazil are sometimes not given the attention they deserve in North American academic circles. Still, the influx of scientists from the north did expand the knowledge base and also focused attention on the issues of most concern up north.

For practical purposes, there were a few major questions that bee-keepers and public officials in the United States wanted addressed. How had the Africanized bees migrated so far from their starting point in southern Brazil? Why did most of the European bees in their path become Africanized, while the Africanized bees continued to be as nasty as ever? How far into a temperate, non-tropical setting could these tropically-oriented insects establish themselves? Would they be as bad in the United States as they were in Latin America? Researchers made fairly good progress on the first couple of questions, but there is still considerable debate over the last two.

What the researchers found was that the descendants of *Apis mellifera scutellata* were having a wonderful time in their new territory. The Brazilians had wanted a bee that was better suited to the tropics than the European bee, and they got one. The European honey bee had performed poorly and had never established much of a feral population in the tropics, because it was not adaptable to that environment. The European honey bee subspecies acted on cues from variations in sunlight and temperature that signalled a change of season. They were also a bit particular in foraging choices and selective about where they put their nesting sites. By contrast, the Africanized bees brought into play behavior that had helped the *scutellata* subspecies survive for thousands of years back in Africa, where unpredictable conditions were the norm. The lack of a wild European population in the Latin American tropics also meant that the Africanized bees were the only game in town, having no real competition for resources.

Once the Africanized bees had established a good sized feral population in an area where managed European hives were present, another advantage came into play. Africanized bees produce far more drones than do Europeans. In an experiment conducted by USDA researchers in Venezuela during the mid-1980s, two apiaries were established with equal numbers of European and Africanized colonies. Within a short time, over 90 percent of the drones tested in each apiary were found to be Africanized.

The drones carry only the maternal genes, since they are produced from unfertilized eggs, so, over time, hybrid-by-hybrid matings in the wilds of South America, where there was no genetic competition, favored an increase in African characteristics. When these feral colonies built up in large numbers around a managed apiary, they had so many drones flying out to mate that it was only a matter of time before the apiary bees became Africanized, too.

The Africanized bees also amplified their reproductive edge through a couple of little tricks. Scientists observed the Africanized bees directly taking over hives already occupied by European bees. First a small cluster of invading bees, containing an Africanized queen, would enter the hive. Then, the little Africanized storm troopers would find the European queen and kill her, replacing her with their own queen. Within a matter of weeks, the hive would be completely Africanized. Another action was dubbed "drone parasitism." Some of the excess Africanized drones would leave their own colonies and take up residence in European colonies, thereby displacing the European drones and putting even more Africanized drones into the mating pool.

Some researchers thought that there might be other factors as well. They found evidence that Africanized queens were mating almost exclusively with Africanized drones, while European colonies seemed to have little impact on the genetic characteristics of the Africanized bees. This led to speculation about differences in mating flight times or possible mating preferences particular to each subspecies, but other scientists said these differences, even if they did exist, probably were of little consequence compared to the Africanized bees' overall advantage in drone numbers. In any case, they found it is not easy to study the sex lives of insects who mate as they fly through the air, 1,200 feet up, at a speed of 14 miles an hour!

Buzzing onward!

The movement of the bees from southern Brazil to other parts of the continent was a fascinating spectacle. The wave of bees moved like a storm front across the South American terrain. Within the first 15 years after the alleged "escape" at Rio Claro, the Africanized bees had occupied an area in South America as large as the continental United States. In three decades, the bees would spread over some eight million square miles of South and Central America, producing billions of bees in the process.

The migration was mainly driven by reproductive swarms. There are two basic types of swarms: a prime swarm, in which the "old" queen takes off with about half of the colony, leaving behind several capped queen cells, from which a new queen will emerge within a matter of days; and afterswarms, in which new-born, virgin queens emerge, and within a few days, fly off with a retinue of workers and drones. These swarms typically consist of a few thousand bees and a queen, although at certain times, there can be small swarms with not much more than a handful of bees. They are called reproductive swarms, because more queen bees mean more swarms, and more swarms mean more colonies with a queen laying eggs to make more bees.

European bees, in temperate climates, swarm in the spring and sometimes the fall. Africanized bees, in the tropics, swarm in the dry season, which can last several months. European bee swarms usually do not travel more than a mile or two from the starting point because the bees are surviving on the honey they slurped up just before leaving. Once their little bellies are getting empty, they need to start setting up a new home. Africanized bees, on the other hand, travel up to 100 miles, stopping frequently along the way to exploit good foraging opportunities, in order to replenish themselves before moving on again.

Whereas a European colony may produce one or two swarms a year, researchers in French Guiana observed that a normal colony of Africanized bees sent out around 12 swarms during the dry season, which lasted from July to February. They estimated that one colony and the swarms it produced could eventually create a total of 64 swarms in a season! Sometimes the swarms would coincide in their flight path, creating a flying cloud of bees containing multiple queens. This was not totally unexpected, since in Africa there had been numerous observations of giant "megaswarms," containing up to 500 mated queens and enough bees to fill a 160 gallon container.

The high reproductive rate of the Africanized bees, and their frenetic issuance of swarms, followed their general pattern of hyperactivity. Entomological investigators noticed that while European bees would enter a hive box by first landing at the entrance and then walking in, the Africanized bees flew directly in. When foraging, the Africanized bees literally worked themselves to death. European worker bees generally live for more than a month during the foraging season, but studies showed that the Africanized bees in South America lasted only 12 to 18 days. Their metabolism in general was higher and their wings beat faster. In fact, this led to the development of a device known as a "buzz-buster" for testing Africanization. A bee would be placed in a small chamber connected to an electronic apparatus that measured the hum of the rapidly moving wings. Africanized bees, on average, beat their little wings 50 times more per second than do Europeans.

Researchers also found that the migrating bees in South America had sometimes been "given a lift" by humans. Often, it happened by accident, when swarms got into a truck or boat and were inadvertently transported to another area. More serious, however, were accidental movements of these bees by beekeepers, who would introduce the African strain into previously untainted apiaries. In Peru, for example, Africanized bees had been stopped by the high Andes mountains from passing over to the Pacific coast, leaving that part of Peru and all of Chile and Ecuador free of the problem. But in the late 1970s, beekeepers in Peru's northern coastal area began noticing a sharp increase in the aggressiveness of their bees. Tests later indicated that the African genes had mixed into the bees of many managed hives and that feral Africanized colonies had even spread northward along the coastal plain into Ecuador. Investigators were able to trace the problem to two beekeepers from Chulucanas, in Peru's northwestern province of Piura, who in 1978 had purchased 300 colonies of bees from an area in southeastern Peru that had been infested with Africanized bees. They then transported these hives over the Andes, bringing Africanized bees to an area they probably wouldn't have reached on their own.

Human reaction to the fiery-tempered bees also sometimes aided the Africanization process. In most areas, when the first feral swarms arrived, local beekeepers paid little notice. When the stinging incidents began, however, many of them abandoned their colonies, allowing them to be taken over by the invading bees. Some of the better-prepared, better-educated, and better-financed beekeepers were able to adapt by requeening their colonies with certified European stock and by developing methods to cope with the highly defensive bees — but it was not easy and it was also expensive.

Mapping the Beeline

After following the Africanized bees through French Guiana, Venezuela and part of Central America, Orley Taylor, an entomology professor from the University of Kansas, estimated their rate of migration northward at around 200 to 300 miles a year. The rate would vary, depending on the terrain, the climatic conditions, and other factors. The bees seemed to move faster over dry, savanna-like tropical zones. Areas with heavy rainfall, on the other hand, slowed them down. Taylor produced a map with predicted dates of arrival at various points. He said they would probably reach the United States, through southern Texas, by 1988 or early 1989. Of course, this was an estimate based on their movement, up to that time, through tropical regions, and Taylor had to revise his predictions later. The map, however, proved useful for planning purposes and also helped make it clear to officials in the United States that time was running out.

At this point, several researchers, including Taylor, were noticing an interesting pattern. Major stinging incidents generally did not begin to happen for a year or two after the first swarms arrived. Some bee experts speculated that this indicated the existence of "pioneer swarms" which formed the migrating front and which were more prone towards mobility than defense. There was also the likelihood that the bees became super-defensive only after they had settled in and built up a large population. The other thing that investigators noticed was that, after the first few bad years, stinging incidents subsided. Some researchers assumed this was partly a result of public awareness of the problem, but there was also a suspicion that hybridization might be playing a role in reducing the defensiveness of the bees.

The question of genetic dilution was also important for determining how well the tropical insects would do in the colder climate of North America. Orley Taylor's maps showed the Africanized bees advancing up into south Texas and into some other southern states, but not going much farther north. Based on his studies of the bees in more temperate zones in South America, he predicted they would inhabit only the extreme southern regions of the United States, where winters are mild. This, however, soon became the focus of another debate. As will be discussed in Chapter Six, some

Spread of the Africanized Honey Bee

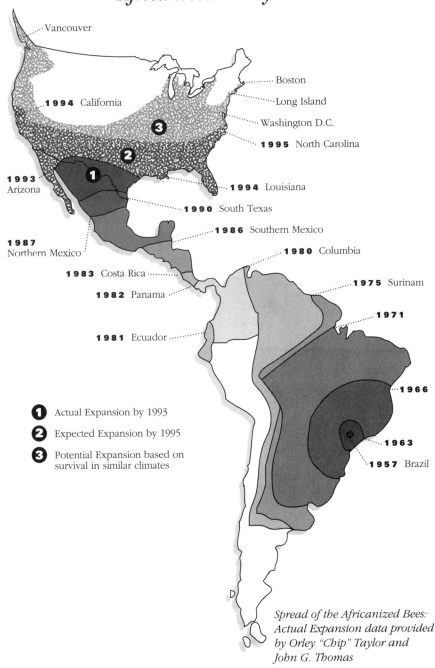

Vancouver

Boston
Long Island
Washington D.C.

1994 California

1995 North Carolina

❸

❷

1993
Arizona

❶

1994 Louisiana

1990 South Texas

1986 Southern Mexico

1987
Northern Mexico

1980 Columbia

1983 Costa Rica

1975 Surinam

1982 Panama

1971

1981 Ecuador

1966

❶ Actual Expansion by 1993

❷ Expected Expansion by 1995

1963

❸ Potential Expansion based on
survival in similar climates

1957 Brazil

*Spread of the Africanized Bees:
Actual Expansion data provided
by Orley "Chip" Taylor and
John G. Thomas*

researchers saw no reason why it would not be possible for the Africanized bees to make it all the way to Canada!

At this point, Canadian agriculture officials and beekeepers developed a plan to cope with the threat, just in case. Although they did not expect the Africanized bees to migrate to their country any time soon, Canadians were concerned that even Taylor's more conservative predictions showed the combative bees reaching areas in the American South where there were many queen breeders and package bee suppliers who serviced Canadian customers. This threat of Africanization also came on top of a bee mite infestation in the United States that Canadians dearly wished to avoid. So, long before any Africanized bee had even entered U.S. territory, Canada had already developed methods to overwinter colonies and to rear queens, so that imports from the United States would not be necessary. In 1987, with its program already in place, Canada prohibited any further import of bees from the United States. This advanced planning provided an interesting contrast with the Latin American nations, where there was generally a response only after the Africanized front had arrived and had begun causing trouble.

One tropical nation that did try to hold back the bees was Trinidad and Tobago, a Caribbean island country, which is separated from Venezuela by the narrow gulf of Paria. Africanized swarms began flying the eight and a half miles across the water to the island of Trinidad in the late 1970s. The government then initiated a program to find and destroy feral honey bee colonies, while European stock was maintained through frequent revision. Eventually, the Africanized bees won the war, but the Trinidadians succeeded in delaying their complete victory by as much as four and a half years.

The Panama story

Another nation that made a concentrated effort to deal with the African menace was Panama. This narrow, isthmian nation had two concerns: the Panama Canal, through which ships from every part of the world pass on an almost daily basis, and a small, but growing honey production sector. The first swarm of Africanized bees in Panama was found, in January of 1982, by Alberto Silva, an apiary inspector and small beekeeper, in the eastern province of Darien. The Panama City-based Smithsonian Tropical Research Institute's resident bee expert, David Roubik, used morphometric measurements, that is, measurements of certain body parts, to confirm the bees as Africanized.

Shortly after that, the Panamanian government established a commission to deal with the problem. It included government officials, as well as the Tropical Research Institute and beekeepers. At the same time, the Panama Canal Commission and nearby U.S. military bases developed their own control programs. It was a losing battle, in terms of stopping the bees from occupying Panama. In little more than a year, the migration made it all the way from Darien to the Costa Rican border at the other end of the country. The program did succeed, however, in alerting the public to the danger, thereby preventing needless death and injury; and it did prevent, to some extent, the international waterway and ports from being utilized by the bees as a launching pad for trips to other regions of the world.

As part of his involvement in the control programs, David Roubik joined Canal Commission entomologist Melvin Boreham to conduct a study of the incoming bees, finding them to be, in size and in other characteristics, very similar to the pure *scutellata* bees of Africa. Having had few European bees with which to inter-breed in eastern Panama, the bees maintained their African traits as they moved forward to the canal area. The defensiveness of the bees seemed strong as ever. Peasants and canal personnel who accidentally disturbed colonies in the bush often fell victim to massive attacks. In one case, some canal workers disrupted a colony of Africanized bees who had nested in a hollow palm tree. The bees severely stung three of them, with one man going to the hospital for several days to be treated for more than 1,000 stings.

One reason for stinging incidents, Roubik and Boreham found, was that people had no way of predicting where they would be likely to come across the bees. There had been very few honey bee colonies in Panama before the African invasion, and most had been kept in apiaries far from population centers. The Africanized bees, however, quickly built a wild population and took advantage of every imaginable nesting site. Only 26 percent of the bee nests found in the canal zone area during the 48-month study period were in natural settings. Of the others, 32 percent were found in such places as school buildings, warehouses, athletic stadiums and power plants; and 41 percent were located in such miscellaneous sites as water meter boxes, utility manholes, light poles, empty oil drums, pipes, and air conditioner ducts. Often, Roubik and Boreham found, the Africanized bees established large nests that were open and exposed to a wide variety of possible disturbances. Unlike swarms, which will often rest for a period of days in open clusters and are docile, the nesting bees had produced honeycomb to defend and would do so at the slightest provocation.

Over the 48 months of the Roubik and Boreham study, the Panama Canal Commission teams destroyed 1,175 bee colonies in various areas along the waterway and in nearby industrial, residential, and recreational areas. During the same period, the U.S. military teams took care of almost 1,000 colonies on bases near the canal, and Panama City firemen were called on to eliminate several thousand more colonies within the urban zone.

The impact on beekeeping in Panama was severe. There was an 80 percent drop in the number of maintained honey bee colonies in Panama during the first several years after the Africanized bees arrived in 1982. Beekeeping had only recently begun to expand in Panama and was seeing real growth right up until 1982. As had been the case in other countries to the south, beekeeping had been officially encouraged as an agricultural development activity and as a means of creating employment and income. In 1982, Panama produced its largest ever honey crop: 174,448 gallons. There were 369 beekeepers spread out over the countryside, maintaining 21,806 colonies. Panama had also developed an export market in Europe for its honey, shipping out more than 150 tons to Switzerland and Germany. By the end of the decade, the export market was gone, only 179 beekeepers remained, working 3,613 colonies. Overall honey production had fallen to 18,693 gallons, the lowest it had been since the early 1970s, when the drive to increase beekeeping activity in Panama was just getting started.

The Panama story is similar to those of other Latin American nations, where part of the cost of Africanization has been the dashed hopes of poor, rural people trying to eke out a better standard of living for themselves and their families. The devastation of these fledgling beekeeping industries sent a strong alarm to the nations of North America, where beekeeping was already well-established as an important, if not a vital, part of agricultural enterprise.

Ecological Impact

HOW IS THE ECOLOGICAL BALANCE EFFECTED WHEN A SPECIES which previously did not exist, or existed in very limited numbers, in a given area suddenly invades and, within a few years, establishes a large population? Very little is known about the Africanized honey bee's ecological impact on the vast areas of tropical forest and dry savanna which it has occupied in the last three decades. Among the intriguing questions is whether the influx of these honey bees has, in any way, displaced or disrupted the indigenous pollinators, and if so, what impact that has had on plants requiring pollination. More than half of the plants in a forest that produce food for wildlife require pollination. Any disruption in pollination could have consequences on down the food chain.

Photos above: Bee swarms. The AHB swarms frequently producing many feral colonies. Photos by Norman Gary, Dept. of Entomology, UC Davis

Gerald Loper, a USDA researcher who has conducted studies of Africanized bee drone abatement measures in Costa Rica, says he has seen evidence of tropical bird nests being taken over by swarms of migrating bees. He and other researchers who have noticed such displacement of wild animals wonder what the long term impact could be on the wildlife population. No specific studies have been done on this yet.

The most immediate impact of Africanized honey bees that could be expected in tropical America would be on other species of bees, namely the stingless *Melipona* and *Trigona*, which are indigenous to most of the areas that the Africanized bees have now made their home and must compete for resources with the invaders. David Roubik has conducted studies in three areas of Latin America to determine if the native bees have been adversely effected by the invasion. He started one study in French Guiana more than 15 years ago and another in Mexico's Yucatan peninsula a little over five years ago. More recently, he has done some preliminary impact studies on Barro Colorado Island, which is located in Gatun Lake, in the middle of the Panama Canal and is maintained by the Smithsonian Tropical Research Institute.

On Barro Colorado Island, Roubik found ample evidence of Africanized bee saturation, but the preliminary results do not show any sign of the native stingless bees declining in population as a result. In both French Guiana and the Yucatan, however, he did find worrisome signs that the African-derived honey bees are displacing the indigenous bee species.

The Maya Indians who live in the Yucatan area have been harvesting honey from the *Melipona* bees for over a thousand years and while some people now manage

European honey bees and Africanized honey bees, the sting-less bee honey harvests are still an important tradition. In 1990, Roubik noticed, that for the first time in anyone's memory, the stingless bee colonies had grown weak and had not produced any surplus honey.

"There wasn't any drought, there wasn't any fire," says Roubik. "There was nothing you could put your finger on to explain this, but there certainly was a noticeable increase in the numbers of swarms and feral colonies of honey bees, all of which were Africanized."

Roubik says this kind of study takes many years to complete, but he says there is strong evidence to suggest that the influx of Africanized honey bees has contributed to a decline in the native bees. He says this is mostly because of the massive numbers of workers the feral honey bee colonies can send out to exploit nectar sources, at the expense of the native bees. A feral Africanized colony may have 30,000 bees at work, whereas a stingless bee colony has only around 5,000. Roubik describes honey bee colonies as "foraging machines," which can have an especially profound impact on areas where food sources are limited. He believes the Yucatan is one such area.

"The days are numbered for the stingless bees there," he says.

Besides their advantage in numbers, Roubik says, the Africanized honey bees also have an advantage in their complex communication system, whereby scout bees will return to the hive and perform a complicated dance to "tell" the other bees about a foraging opportunity that they can then go out to exploit immediately in large numbers. Another factor that Roubik thinks may play a part in this is the ability of the

African-derived bees to coalesce into even larger colonies. He says feral Africanized swarms with as many as 100,000 bees have been found in Latin America.

Roubik sees some irony in the possible displacement of the native stingless bees by the Africanized bees in parts of tropical America, since the man who introduced the African honey bees, Warwick Kerr, has devoted most of his professional life to working with the stingless bees in the Amazon rainforests. Roubik says it will undoubtedly pain Kerr to think that the bees he introduced from Africa are, in Roubik's view "slowly, but surely causing the extinction of the bees he began studying, in the place he began studying them."

CHAPTER FIVE

"The Bee Barrier"

WHEN BEEKEEPERS AND AGRICULTURAL EXPERTS IN THE United States began to realize the potential threat from Africanized bees and when some public officials, especially in those states that would likely feel the first effects, began to heed the warnings, plans started percolating to stop the migrating horde somewhere south of the border. By the time such discussion got underway, the Africanized bees had already kicked up a storm in the northern part of South America and were headed into Panama. The dense Darien jungle, on the eastern edge of the isthmus of Panama, is a natural biological barrier for many species but it was just one more inviting opportunity for these bees. There was some talk of spraying massive amounts of insecticides in the area, but that would have killed indiscriminately and would have created an ecological disaster far worse than any imaginable threat from the bees.

While the pipe dreaming continued, the Africanized bees moved on through Panama, Costa Rica, Nicaragua, Honduras, El Salvador, Belize and Guatemala. In each country, the results were similar, a drop of 40 to 60 percent in honey production, abandonment of managed colonies by those less willing or less able to cope, and a sharp increase in stinging incidents. There was no effort made to stop the bees in Central America, however, because there was no workable plan and no money to implement one. Another problem would have been getting cooperation from nations who would have to invest precious time, resources, and territory to an effort that would basically benefit the United States. None of these nations had an important beekeeping industry to defend.

Mexico, on the other hand, did have a well-developed honey production sector and experts there watched the approach of the Africanized bees with concern. Mexico was the first nation in the path of the Africanized bees to begin planning for them years in advance of their arrival. The Mexican government's program, administered by the Agriculture Ministry, known by its acronym SARH (*Secretaria de Agricultura y Recursos Hidraulicos*), started by gathering information from experts in the Latin American nations that had already felt the wrath of the African bloodline. The Mexicans then set up an educational program to prepare campesinos, beekeepers, and the public in general. They also took an important step in setting up trap lines along the border with Guatemala, where the first entry of the bees was expected.

Long before the bees began entering southern Mexico, USDA officials, in discussion with their Mexican counterparts, had begun work on a plan to establish a biological barrier at Mexico's narrowest point, the 150-mile-wide Isthmus of Tehuantepec. This area had been used before to arrest the spread of troublesome pests, most notably the screw worm fly, a nasty little number that infests animals and, in some cases, humans, with a larva (maggot) that feeds on the living flesh found in open wounds. The screw worm had been eliminated from the United States by the 1970s and, in a cooperative effort, U.S. and Mexican agricultural officials pushed the pests farther and farther south until a barrier could be established at Tehuantepec.

The agriculture experts attacked the screw worm flies biologically. First, they established quarantines to keep cattle infested with the larvae from moving to other areas. Then, millions of sterile male flies were broadcast from small airplanes over infested areas. Little by little, the screw worm problem was eliminated because the flood of sterile flies overwhelmed the wild population of fertile male flies and reproduction was reduced to practically nothing. The program worked so well that farmers below the barrier line asked to be included and new programs were begun to eliminate the flies from southern Mexico and Central America. The program is still underway in Central America and officials hope to push the barrier to the afore-mentioned Darien region in Panama within the next several years.

Of course, bees are not flies. While officials could eliminate flies with impunity, they could not target bees in general without destroying the very beekeeping industry they were trying to protect. What was needed were measures that would control Africanized bees while not doing harm to European bees.

The Strategy

In 1985, USDA researchers came up with a plan to establish what they called a "Bee Regulated Zone," or BRZ, in the Tehuantepec region. It was to be a barrier not to bees, but to the undesirable characteristics of the Africanized bees. The hope was that a variety of tactics combined at one point might hold back the mass migration and allow time for genetic dilution of bees passing into the zone.

The first basic component of the BRZ plan was a quarantine, to regulate the movement of colonies from below the barrier to other areas. The plan relied, to some extent, on measures already in place in southern Mexico to control screw worms and other agricultural pests. In addition to checkpoints on roadways, there would be training for Mexican inspection teams already operating at ports, so they would know how to check docking ships for the presence of Africanized bees.

In order to deal with the frequent swarms from the Africanized front, the USDA plan called for baited hives to attract swarms, which could then be enclosed and either destroyed or carted off for study. These traps were to consist of a simple cardboard box, partially covered with a plastic bag to protect it from rain, which could be hung from a tree. A scent of bee pheromone or traces of beeswax would be used to attract the bees. In addition to the traps, the BRZ plan called for collecting samples from the wild and from managed apiaries, so that inroads by the migrating Africanized bees could be quickly spotted and dealt with.

In order to counter the Africanized tendency to send out a cluster of workers with a queen to take over European hives, the BRZ planners looked to putting queen excluders on managed European hive boxes and placing traps to catch swarms in the vicinity of apiaries. In order for these measures to work, rural Mexican beekeepers would have to give up their rustic hives, which often consisted of small hollow logs. They would have to be replaced with modern moveable-frame hives provided to the beekeepers by the BRZ program. The beekeepers would also have to be encouraged to check their colonies frequently to make sure that there was a queen and that, if so, she was European. European queens could be marked with a dot of enamel paint on the back of the thorax for easy identification. Any queen that did not have this mark would be a suspected invader and would have to be destroyed. Some of these same measures would help prevent another problem, that of Africanized drones entering European colonies. Drone traps could also be placed near apiaries to capture invading drones from feral Africanized colonies. Of course, this part of the plan would depend heavily on complete cooperation from the beekeepers in the area.

Absconding Africanized swarms entering the BRZ would be targeted by placing special traps in the area and by paying a bounty to local campesinos who would report the presence of swarms to the BRZ team. Since research in Kenya had shown that absconding swarms of African bees stopped every 20 miles or so to spend a few days foraging for nectar and pollen, there was a chance that most swarms flying across the barrier could be captured with the baited traps. Of course, nothing of this sort could ever be 100 percent effective, but the idea was to reduce the numbers of invading Africanized bees to a point where the large population of European bees in the area could hold its own.

For the Europeans to stand up to even a diminished invasion of Africanized bees, however, the BRZ team would have to deal with the mating advantages of the African bee line. That meant finding a way to control the large numbers of drones produced by the many feral swarms of Africanized bees entering the area. An important approach to this problem, in the opinion of the authors, was to encourage production of more drones in managed European colonies within the zone.

The ambitious BRZ plan had a projected budget of $8 million. This would pay for a headquarters operation in Mexico and, among other things, 140,800 bait stations, 140,800 bait hives, 220 vehicles and 88 work sites. In addition, there would be 1,144 employees, mostly Mexican field workers. Half the cost was to be shared by Mexico and, in addition, Mexican officials were to provide other support services in the field.

In September of 1986, the first confirmed swarm of Africanized honey bees to enter Mexico was found just over the border from Guatemala at the Pacific coast town of Ciudad Hidalgo. (By coincidence, Hidalgo was also the name of the town in Texas where the first confirmed swarm from the overland migration into the United States would be found in October of 1990.) In December, the Mexican government made a formal proposal to the United States for a cooperative program to control the Africanized bee invasion in Mexico. As the Africanized swarms spread into the southern state of Chiapas, a team put together by the USDA and SARH began tracking their progress, utilizing a continuously changing map to show the location of the invading bees. What they found was that the bees were moving faster than expected and that the plan to hold them off at Tehuantepec was already in trouble.

The Battlefield

The first shots fired in the war on the Africanized bees in Mexico came from researchers and apiculture experts who derided the government plan as "an insect Maginot line" or "a barbed wire fence for bees." One news magazine featured a derisive cartoon showing a bee nuzzling up against a Berlin-style wall. Many experts in academia thought the money could be spent better on direct research since they saw the whole concept of a barrier as flawed from the start.

Cornell's Roger Morse called the idea "humbug" and a waste of taxpayers' money. He regarded the USDA plan to alter the Africanized bees genetically by maintaining a large amount of European stock in the BRZ as a forlorn hope lacking any scientific basis. "To talk of genetic dilution is ridiculous," said Morse. "It has not happened in the 31 years since the bees arrived in Brazil and there is no reason to think it will happen in Mexico."

Orley Taylor also derided the plan to establish a genetic front. His studies had shown that the migrating Africanized bees had changed very little in terms of their genetic characteristics and he saw little hope that human intervention at the bee barrier would dilute their African blood. "We cannot Europeanize these bees," he said. "They are going to reach us essentially unchanged."

While Taylor, Morse and some of the other experts criticized the project, they were, nonetheless, cooperative, providing useful information to the USDA team in Mexico. There were also some academic researchers who supported the plan and felt it had at least some chance of success. Some of the researchers believed that the BRZ could prove useful if only in delaying the bees. Others saw it as an opportunity to study the dynamics of the bee migration up close with the help of a large team that no academic institution could ever have afforded to assemble with its own resources.

Of course, by the time the plan was ready to be implemented, it was only a shadow of what had originally been contemplated. The scientific naysayers had convinced many members of the U.S. Congress that money spent on a bee barrier would be wasted. Besides, the whole "killer bee" issue had gotten so distorted by science fiction writers and television comics that some Congressmen probably felt that funding for the BRZ would be as easy to defend as funding for a defense against UFO's. Even after Congress approved a modified plan, there were bureaucratic delays which held up implementation.   ·

By the summer of 1987, the Africanized bees, helped by strong winds, had already moved into the Isthmus of Tehuantepec and any hope of establishing an effective barrier there had to be abandoned. So, a scaled-down approach was implemented, with two operational units being established just north of the isthmus on each coast, utilizing the mountains through the middle as a natural dividing point, since honey bees normally do not move up to nest in higher elevations on their own. The primary operational unit was centered at Puerto Escondido, on the Pacific coast of the state of Oaxaca. It was rectangular in shape and was approximately 22 miles wide and 34 miles long. The second operational unit was set up near Veracruz. It was triangular in shape; about 50 miles wide at the base and 80 miles long on each side. Establishment of the second unit was made necessary by an unexpected turn northward by the migrating bees when they reached the Isthmus of Tehuantepec. Strong winds that blew down about half of the bait traps in the area also helped carry the bees from their path along the Pacific coast, across the open fields of Tehuantepec towards the Gulf coast. Africanized swarms coming up through Guatemala's Peten region and neighboring Belize were also expected to reach the Yucatan area and the Gulf of Mexico, but much later.

Instead of being a barrier, the control area was to be a sort of zone of resistance to slow the migration and to produce as much hybridization as possible to reduce the aggressiveness of the bees. Beekeepers would maintain their colonies within the operational units and efforts would be directed at protecting those colonies from Africanization. At the same time, traps would be set to capture as many incoming Africanized swarms as possible. The beekeepers would also be encouraged to produce more drones to offset the African mating advantage by "flooding" the operational units with European drones. Instead of $8 million, the program had about $3 million for the first year, with half of that coming from the United States and the other half coming from Mexico. Instead of counting on more than a thousand employees, the program had 141 field workers, who mostly checked traps. There were also two researchers, two accountants, two public relations representatives and two co-directors. In each set of two, one was American and the other Mexican.

The U.S. director of the project in Mexico was a Japanese-American from Hawaii, Ralph Iwamoto, who worked for USDA's Animal and Plant Health Inspection Service, known as APHIS. His counterpart was Gustavo Rodriguez from SARH. They followed the movement of the bees on large maps and met frequently, as would allied generals cooperating in a war against a common enemy. Although the two men had a good working relationship, their two governments were not always in the best coordination. Some off-the-road vehicles from the United States that were to have been used by the field workers in remote areas were held up by Mexican customs for so long that they were of little use when they finally did arrive. For a time, the Mexicans also refused to allow European queens from U.S. apiaries to be brought in for requeening hives because of mite infestations in the United States.

The cultural climate of Mexican bureaucracy sometimes clashed with Ralph Iwamoto's sense of how things should be done. He says Mexican officials hired field workers, but sometimes failed to provide the gasoline for the vehicles to take them to the field. Mexican officials, Iwamoto found, had a tendency to put a lot of emphasis on statistics, such as the number of traps placed in an area and the number of swarms captured. He says these figures were often meaningless because they were so exaggerated. He also found that the Mexican bookkeeping was a bit loose and that funds that were supposed to be used on the cooperative effort sometimes paid salaries and other expenses for the Mexican national program.

The cross-cultural misunderstandings extended to the work in the field, where Mexican workers, who were getting a salary from the program, also wanted to receive a bounty for each swarm they found in a baited trap. There was a one dollar bonus for workers who captured feral swarms they found in the field, but not for the ones that were found in the program's own traps. Iwamoto also found that the field workers had a tendency to place traps in highly-visible areas, along roadways, for example, which sometimes did more to advertise the program than it did to trap bees.

The biggest problem, though, came from the local beekeepers. If there was one key element in the revised plan for the Bee Regulated Zone, it was the maintenance of European stock in local apiaries to offset the feral Africanized colonies arriving in the area. But Ralph Iwamoto says the Mexican beekeepers did not always view the program as something that would benefit them. Iwamoto and his Mexican counterparts spent considerable time talking with beekeepers and beekeeper associations in southern Mexico trying to get everyone on board but there were many who had a mind of their own about the whole issue.

"We did not realize that the beekeepers would not cooperate," Iwamoto says. "On paper, everything worked out and we had the cooperation of all these beekeepers. On paper it looked good, but when the time came for beekeepers to cooperate, they didn't."

One thing the cooperative program team did not count on was the rivalry that existed between some beekeepers' associations, with some supporting the program and others opposing it. Some large scale beekeepers viewed the Africanized bee as potentially beneficial and welcomed their arrival. Some smaller operators took a fatalistic attitude, saying that if they couldn't handle the invading bees, they would just drop beekeeping and find something else to do. An anthropologist with knowledge of Mexican rural conditions and cultural dynamics might have been useful to the team but it is doubtful that anyone could have gotten full cooperation from all the beekeepers.

The fatal flaw in the program was that there was no money to compensate beekeepers for losses they might incur. Being independent types by nature, beekeepers resented government interference in their business, especially if it would cost them money. The cooperative program team wanted to keep all managed colonies within the two operational units all year long. The beekeepers, however, traditionally moved colonies up the mountainsides every dry season (winter) to take advantage of the nectar flow. The bee team offered them sugar water and protein to keep their colonies alive, but this could hardly compare with a potentially profitable honey harvest. So, many of them moved their colonies up the mountain slopes and the whole system of control fell apart.

The Outcome

Ralph Iwamoto still clings to the idea that the cooperative program might have worked as a real genetic barrier had it been supported through more funding. In one year alone, he notes, the screw worm cooperative program got $32 million from the U.S. Congress, whereas the amount appropriated for the Africanized honey bee cooperative program during its four years of existence was just over $1.5 million annually. Iwamoto is among those who believe that the program did succeed in slowing the African migration by as much as two years. Even many of the researchers who originally criticized the plan now credit it for having provided some valuable scientific data on the bees and for having been a pilot project, in a sense, for the development of management programs farther north.

Thomas Rinderer, a USDA insect geneticist who was instrumental in developing the original BRZ plan, also believes the barrier concept might have worked if it had been properly supported. "We would be chasing them down through Venezuela now," he jokes.

Though he is reluctant to play the game of hindsight, Rinderer says more money would have helped. Had the program been able to compensate the Mexican beekeepers, he says, the Africanized front would have had more European drones in its path and there would have been more hybridization as a result. As it turned out, he says, the bees were slowed considerably, arriving in the United States later than some researchers, notably Orley Taylor, had predicted. Rinderer says the lack of a strict control component makes it difficult to say with certainty that the cooperative program accomplished this delay, rather than say, weather patterns, but he says, with a wry chuckle, "you might as well give the people in the program credit because that is what they were trying to do."

Rinderer also believes the cooperative program in Mexico succeeded in reducing the undesirable traits of the Africanized bees by creating a broad range of hybrids within the migrating front. He says the bees now moving through northern Mexico and Texas are "...clearly, in the main, pretty substantially hybridized." Orley Taylor and some other researchers take exception on that point, based on their DNA studies that show bees at the migrating front to be almost pure *scutellata* types, but only time and a lot more research studies will settle the issue.

One thing the cooperative effort clearly did was help Mexico enhance its national education program to warn and inform people about the bees. Through television commercials, posters and cartoon booklets, Mexican officials have underscored the positive aspects of bees and beekeeping while warning people not to mess with the little creatures. The African bee has been portrayed in cartoons developed by SARH as a little African warrior, fierce but lovable. The main motif features a cute and cuddly little

Top: "Hello, I am the Africanized Bee"
Bottom: "We do not like it when you disturb us"
Secretaria de Agricultura y Recursos Hidraulicos (Mexican Agriculture Ministry)

honey bee saying, *"Cuidame,"* Spanish for "Take care of me." Although there have been a few dozen deaths attributed to Africanized bees in Mexico, stinging incidents of the magnitude experienced in South America have been avoided partly because most people in rural Mexico now know what to expect from these bees and how to avoid any unpleasant encounter with them. Whereas beekeeping in some parts of southern Mexico was almost devastated by the influx of Africanized bees, better-equipped and better-prepared beekeepers in other parts of the country have fared well.

Miel Carlota, one of Mexico's biggest honey production operations, maintains colonies right in the middle of the city of Cuernavaca and although Africanized bees have entered the area, there has been no appreciable drop in production and no serious public incident. Beekeepers have learned how to keep colonies in areas away from the public and how to requeen colonies to keep African influence out. Mexican honey production, so far, has not diminished significantly as a result of the bee invasion.

The Mexican government has continued its cooperation with USDA in conducting studies of the Africanized bees as they move farther north and much of what is being learned informs the planning going on in border states today. Although some gringos may dream wistfully of the barrier that might have been, Mexican officials tend not to dwell much on the failure to halt the migration of the Africanized bees. Salvador Cajero, who heads the Mexican Agriculture Ministry's current bee program, emphasizes instead the practical knowledge that has been gained and the ongoing efforts to protect the nation's honey production. Asked if any kind of bee barrier could have worked, he says, "It is impossible to stop these bees."

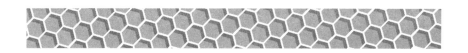

CHAPTER SIX

The African Genes

AS THE AFRICANIZED SWARMS PROLIFERATED AND CONTINUED their migration up the two coastlines of Mexico, the debate over what impact they would have farther north, in the United States, intensified. Some experts, notably Cornell's Roger Morse, took the position that too much fuss was being made about the issue in general. Morse became a beacon of hope to the U.S. beekeeping community by championing the positive aspects of the Africanized bee. He said it was better to accept the fact that the bees were coming and to concentrate on ways of coping with them.

Morse acknowledged the Africanized bees' negative characteristics, but he said beekeepers would be able to work with them. He cited the turnaround in Brazil's beekeeping industry, which, although hard hit at first, recovered and prospered. Morse played music to the ears of many U.S. beekeepers, who feared public and political reaction to the invading bees more than they feared the bees themselves.

Most researchers who had seen the full fury of the bees in Latin America, however, disagreed with Morse's optimistic attitude. They noted that Brazil and some other Latin American nations had paid a high cost, both in deaths and injuries and in lost production, before they managed to recover from the introduction of the African bee. For the beekeepers who were able to survive the onslaught, the work had become much more difficult and expensive. They had to use heavy bee suits and veils when working their colonies, something that was exceedingly uncomfortable in a tropical climate. They also had to find places to maintain apiaries that were far from farm animals and human settlements. Requeening with European stock was another expense, for those that chose that route. In many cases, beekeepers needed to hire extra personnel to help smoke the colonies so that the honey-laden frames could be removed.

USDA researchers were also reluctant to attribute any redeeming qualities to the Africanized bees. Their experiences in the field, mainly in Venezuela, Costa Rica, and Mexico, told them that this was going to be a difficult problem for U.S. beekeeping. They were also skeptical about the productivity of the Africanized bees and questioned how well they would do farther north. Hachiro Shimanuki at USDA's Bee lab in Beltsville, Maryland, believed that U.S. beekeepers would be able to adapt to the bee, but that the general public might not be as patient. People in Latin America are generally more accepting of the trials and disasters nature brings their way, but people in the United States look for someone to blame. Shimanuki said that the first attack by a feral colony of Africanized bees on a toddler "...could spell the end of beekeeping as we know it."

Out in the cold

One debate that began early on, and continues today concerns how far north the Africanized bees will be able to go. After nearly two decades of research, there is still no definitive answer to the question about the Africanized bees' ability to survive in a climate where winters are long and cold. Research has shown that these bees were ideally suited to the tropics and there is a general assumption, on the part of at least some researchers, that they will not be able to overwinter in a colder climate than that which produced them in Africa. Orley Taylor, who developed a map to show the bees' expected range in North America, studied their southern limits in Argentina and concluded that the African progeny were not doing well in the more temperate zones, which begin just north of Buenos Aires. Based on this, he predicted that the Africanized bees would probably not go any farther north than the zones where the mean high temperature in winter is 15 degrees Centigrade (roughly 60 degrees Fahrenheit), or above. This would exclude most of the United States, however, it would include almost half of Texas, and a good portion of California, Arizona, Louisiana, Alabama, Mississippi, Georgia and the Carolinas, as well as the entire state of Florida.

But other researchers have conducted studies that challenge Taylor's idea and suggest that the Africanized bees' overwinter limit could be much farther north. Al Dietz, an entomologist from the University of Georgia, also conducted studies in Argentina and found hybrids that were cold tolerant. He concluded that Africanized bees might be able to survive winters as far north as Boston. USDA research conducted in northern Argentina also indicates that there are hybrid bees with varying degrees of Africanization far into the temperate zones. Further USDA tests in northern Mexico and Texas have shown a similar variety of hybrid bees at the migrating front.

Another element has been contributed by researchers in the original homeland of *Apis mellifera scutellata*, in southern Africa, who pointed out that the bees' habitat is not exclusively tropical. They say these bees have also been found in some relatively cold areas, like the Drakensberg mountains of southeastern South Africa. To test this idea further, USDA researcher Jose Villa conducted a study with Africanized colonies at various elevations in the Andes mountains of Colombia and found that the hybrid bees were able to adapt to the colder climate and higher elevations. His observations led him to conclude that: "The fairly common belief among beekeepers that

Africanized bees are unfit to operate in areas outside truly tropical lowlands needs to be reconsidered."

Researchers have also tried laboratory tests to see if there is any appreciable difference in cold tolerances between Africanized and European bees. One such study was conducted in 1990 by David Roubik and another bee expert, Ed Southwick. They put colonies of both types of bee in enclosed, refrigerated chambers and tested their ability to survive at temperatures slightly above freezing, at freezing, and below freezing.

Roubik says they found both bees could survive the cold:

"We found out that the European and the Africanized bee do exactly the same thing, except that the European bee does it a little bit better. They increase their body metabolism to produce more heat, the colder it gets; and they trap that heat in this tight cluster. The outside layer of bees acts like a fur coat: it keeps some of the heat in. The only problem with the Africanized bees is that they are not as efficient, and they let some of the heat that their bodies make escape. But they maintain their core temperature, just as the European bees do."

Using data from this study, Roubik and Southwick worked with an expert on climate to develop a map showing possible overwintering ranges for the Africanized bees in North America. The range lines went up almost to the Great Lakes area in the midwest, above Washington, DC, on the east coast, and into British Columbia, in Canada, on the west coast.

Today, however, Roubik says he sees many problems with the speculative projection he and his colleagues made. One of the things that he believes must be considered is the high metabolic rate of the Africanized bees. While a European bee can survive in the hive for six months, if necessary, Roubik says there are indications that African bees might not make it more than four months without replenishment. Under conditions of extreme cold, it would probably be less. In addition, he says, not much is known about how wild colonies of

Africanized bees would fare with North American bee predators, such as skunks, badgers and armadillos, who might be all too happy to take advantage of helpless colonies of bees in the dead of winter. For these reasons, and because of the abundance of European bees in the United States, Roubik believes the Africanized bees will not become firmly established in a very large part of the country.

USDA's Thomas Rinderer, who is based at the Agricultural Research Service's Honey Bee Breeding, Genetics and Physiology Research Laboratory in Baton Rouge, Louisiana, agrees that over-wintering is a complex process that involves more than just the ability to withstand cold temperatures. He says the Africanized bees will encounter a limit at some point, but it could be quite far north. He believes they will be able to adapt to varying conditions, just as the *scutellata* bees do in Africa and just as the Africanized bees have done in Latin America. He also believes a combination of mild winters and good foraging opportunities will allow them to live all along the west coast, as far up as British Columbia. Rinderer says it would be as easy for them to live there as it would be for them to live in a southern location like Baton Rouge.

"If you look at plants and their growth characteristics," Rinderer says, "southern British Columbia is in the same zone as Baton Rouge. The climate on the Pacific coast is very muted because of the ocean. There is no substantial winter. It is kind of rainy, but they survive the long rainy season in Venezuela quite well and I see no ecological barrier at all for them on the Pacific side."

Rinderer says the bees coming through Mexico and Texas now are very different from the bees he worked with in South America. He believes exposure to European bees in Mexico, at the BRZ zone and farther north, has created a wide range of hybrids, some of which may be able to overwinter just as efficiently as European bees do.

Herein lies another controversy.

African or Africanized hybrid?

The debate over the northern range and ultimate impact of the Africanized bee has also fueled the debate over just what is an Africanized bee. To determine Africanization, for research purposes, investigators have used a variety of tests, including measurements of honeycomb cells, which are smaller for Africanized bees than they are for European bees (a series of ten cells from a feral European nest ranges from 5.0 to 5.4 cm, while a series of ten cells from an feral Africanized nest ranges from 4.6 to 5.0 cm). Other differences can be found by taking measurements of certain body parts (morphological), DNA analysis of genetic material taken from bee bodies, measurements of metabolic rate, observations of absconding and swarming activity, and tests of defensiveness.

For the average person, and certainly for the beekeeper, the most important tests are behavioral. Are they going to sting? Are they going to run off the frames? Are they going to abscond? These are the practical questions. But behavior tests do not always provide the most accurate determination of heredity, and the same colony can exhibit a wide variety of behavior depending on conditions at the time of the test or observation.

In some early tests conducted in Venezuela by Rinderer and USDA's Anita Collins, alarm pheromone was sprayed in front of a hive and then a black piece of suede was swung in front of the hive entrance to test defensive behavior. (Bees tend to attack dark colored objects more than light ones). The bee stings would remain imbedded in the suede so that they could be counted later. The target was kept at the hive entrance for only 30 seconds in each test. When they did this to European hives, they found that the response was often lackadaisical. Some foraging bees would simply ignore the pheromone, while a few of their sisters flew out to dutifully sacrifice themselves in defense of the colony. With Africanized hives, however, the bees often poured out of the hive by the thousands before the researchers had even gotten completely set up. The Africanized bees implanted more than eight times as many stings in the suede than did European bees, but even that was judged to be an underestimate, since the target became saturated with bees so quickly that not every attacker got her chance!

The researchers also noted that there were variations between the extremes, and that some colonies they knew to be Africanized responded no more viciously than would a normal European colony. They suspected that hybridization was beginning to affect the behavior associated with the Africanized bees. Later studies would show similar results in Central America and Mexico. A study done in Costa Rica in the years following the arrival of the Africanized bees showed a wide range of morphological traits as well as degrees of nervous behavior and defensiveness.

For practical purposes, the USDA needed a method of testing bees for Africanization, not only for research, but also for certifying bee stock in the United States. One item they tried was a test of defensive behavior that employed a black electronic device that could be suspended at a hive entrance to record "hits" from attacking bees. In one field test, an Africanized hive in Costa Rica produced 24 hits per second on the device, as opposed to about four per second from a European hive. This "stingometer" would only give a preliminary indication of Africanization, however, since there are times that European bees get just as nasty as their Africanized relatives. The Agriculture officials settled on a morphological measurement system developed mainly by Thomas Rinderer, which could be used with a fairly high degree of accuracy in the field. It was dubbed FABIS (for Fast Africanized Bee Identification System) and it is still used for initial screening by the USDA today. Here's how it works: Bee samples from a suspect colony are dissected in a lab. The wings, legs and some abdominal areas are carefully measured on a projection screen and the information is then fed into a computer, which gives a percentage probability of Africanization.

Using the Fast Africanized Bee Identification System, Thomas Rinderer checks forewings. Photo courtesy Agricultural Research Service, USDA

Some researchers have used DNA samples taken from bees at the migrating front to demonstrate that the swarms driving the migration are made up of almost purely African bees. In 1989, University of Florida entomology professor H. Glenn Hall did DNA analysis of Africanized bee samples taken at, and behind, the migrating front in Mexico. Using samples of mitochondrial DNA, which is genetic material inherited only from the queen, Hall suggested that bees at the front represent a continuing maternal line of the African *scutellata* race that has not been broken for 150 generations, as the bees migrated over 5,000 miles from Brazil to Mexico. His study suggested that hybrids formed between African bees and European bees do not last, and are replaced over time by bees that are almost pure *scutellata*.

Orley Taylor has carried out similar studies, which show that as the Africa-derived bee swarms reach their territorial limits, there is a hybrid zone that develops, with more pure race Europeans on one side and almost pure African bees on the other. Taylor suggests that the term "Africanized" should not even be used for the bees of the migrating front. "These bees are African," he says. "They are maintaining their genetic integrity."

Thomas Rinderer challenges this notion by pointing to evidence of morphological, biochemical, and behavioral changes in the bees throughout the areas they have occupied in the Americas. Among other evidence, he cites a study done in temperate zones of Argentina by USDA's Steve Sheppard showing that substantial hybridization has existed there since the mid-1970's and that these hybrid populations appear to be stable. Rinderer thinks this and other evidence gathered in the American tropics refutes the idea of the *Apis mellifera scutellata* subspecies maintaining any kind of purity. The USDA geneticist says "Africanized" is the correct term for theses bees since they have many characteristics of *Apis mellifera scutellata*, but also show marked differences which have come about as the result of crossing with European bees. While some colonies are going to be more African-like than others, Rinderer believes that, overall, the Africanized migration coming into the United States now will not be as difficult to handle as the bees he studied in northern Brazil and Venezuela, where the lack of any European colonies with which to inter-breed allowed for backcrosses that produced bees with mostly African characteristics.

"The bees in Venezuela are morphologically the most similar to the bees from Africa," says Rinderer. "The bees that arrived in Venezuela were bees that had gone through northern Brazil, an area where they had no beekeeping, and the Venezuelans did get bees that were pretty much African-like coming into their country from several different directions — at first from along the coast, but later the bees came up from the Amazon into the backside of the country as well."

By contrast, Rinderer says, the bees in Mexico are genetically about half way between the bees from Africa and the European bees. As the invaders breed with the European bees in northern Mexico and the United States, the hybridization should increase. Unfortunately, he says, this will not mean that super-defensiveness will disappear very quickly. "They are not going to be as bad," he says, "but we are not going to get a 'free bee,' either."

How about a Better Bee?

Orley Taylor, meantime, has continued his studies at a site in northern Mexico, where, he says, he has found evidence to support his idea that the African genes come to dominate over time, especially in the feral population. He says the almost pure African wild bees build up their population and then swarm on over to the local bee yard to cause mischief, just as they have done in other parts of Latin America. Taylor says beekeepers can defend their colonies, at least for a while, by producing a flood of European drones around their apiaries.

"Maintaining large numbers of European colonies, or having large numbers of feral (European) colonies is beneficial," he says, "in that it slows down the process of Africanization. You can maintain effective European populations much longer if you have large concentrations of European bees."

The problem, according to Taylor, is that, over time, the African reproductive advantages create a huge feral population that will eventually overwhelm any European bee population, be it feral or managed. Taylor says "there is very strong selection acting on the feral population to eliminate European characteristics."

Orley Taylor expects the process of African dominance to peak in the Rio Grande Valley by 1994. At that point, he says, the feral population will be almost totally Africanized and there will be a

*David Roubik. Photo courtesy of
Smithsonian Institute / C. C. Hansen*

*Orley "Chip" Taylor. Photo courtesy
University of Kansas / M. Frumhoff*

*Roger Morse. Photo courtesy
Charles Harrington, Cornell University
Photography*

*Hachiro Shimanuki. Photo courtesy
Agricultural Research Service, USDA*

potential for worse stinging incidents than have occurred so far. Taylor says public awareness will reduce the danger to average citizens, but he says beekeepers, in spite of their best efforts to protect their colonies through such measures as requeening and drone flooding, may eventually be faced with some hard choices.

"If I am right," Taylor says, "what is going to happen is that, eventually, there will be so many wild bees that the hybridization with the managed bees will simply outstrip the efforts of the beekeepers to manage the situation, or the problem of requeening their colonies is going to be so overwhelming that they will have to make some radical decisions as to whether to continue, or not to continue, or whether to actually start working with the hybrid bees."

Taylor believes many beekeepers in this southern zone may eventually find that the African hybrid bee is a superior bee for their purposes, just as have many beekeepers in Latin America. At that point, he says, the best strategy might be to apply genetic techniques to come up with "a better bee."

An intriguing twist to this idea was proposed by David Fletcher, a biologist from Bucknell University in Pennsylvania who has spent more than 20 years studying bees in southern Africa. He notes that, in Africa, there is a much wider range of defensive behavior among the bees of the *scutellata* subspecies than there appears to be in the Americas. He says there are even some varieties of the bees in Africa which are actually quite mild in temperament and easy to handle. He says the relatively small number of queens introduced to Brazil in 1956 limited the range of genetic characteristics that would be available among the bees in the New World and that, as a result, the "neo-tropical African bees," as he calls them, suffer from an impoverished gene pool that continually produces bees with undesirable behavioral characteristics. So, the answer, Fletcher suggests, is to select some more queens from Africa, based on desirable characteristics, and bring them into the United States to replenish the gene pool. After these new imports have interbred for awhile, Fletcher says, researchers could then take advantage of the variation in the gene pool to selectively breed a gentler and more manageable bee.

As can be imagined, this idea of bringing in more African queens has not been welcomed enthusiastically by federal or state officials, who recall in horror how this whole problem got started in the first place. Nor is the idea embraced by government scientists. In the 1980s USDA researchers did, for a time, consider the possibility of creating a barrier to the Africanized bees by bringing in another African subspecies, *Apis mellifera monticola*, which is a bee more adapted to temperate climates that replaces *scutellata* in the east African highlands. But researchers say any such program would have to be studied and developed very carefully so as to avoid doing more harm than good.

In regard to Fletcher's proposed *scutellata* breeding idea, Thomas Rinderer says that a lot of basic research would have to be done to show that there are strains that would successfully mate with the New World hybrids to produce "a better bee." He says there would also be a danger of what geneticists call "over-dominance," whereby the offspring are more extreme in certain traits than either parent.

"Who knows what you could end up with?" says Rinderer. "You could be creating a strain/hybrid effect that would create bees that are much more deleterious than either of the deleterious parents."

Rinderer thinks there are better ways to challenge the wild and wooly Africanized bees, namely through genetic dilution. Rinderer says that some parts of the United States, especially in the more wooded east, support larger feral European bee colonies than exist anywhere south of the border. He says these wild European bees, combined with the three to four million colonies managed by the more than 200,000 well-experienced U.S. beekeepers, will provide a genetic line of defense stronger than anything yet encountered by the Africanized bees.

In order for beekeepers to maintain manageable colonies in areas where the Africanized bees are building strength, they will have to check their colonies frequently and requeen as necessary. But many queen breeders are located right in the areas where Africanization will probably take hold first. To defend their operations, the queen breeders have two strategies: move some operations to Hawaii, or other locations far from danger, and protect current queen breeding sites through controlled matings. A 1989 USDA study conducted in Texas with two of the nation's biggest queen breeders, Morris and Binford Weaver, showed that it is possible to maintain 90 percent control of matings, which is considered acceptable since studies in Venezuelan apiaries indicated that colonies with 10 percent African/European hybrids displayed manageable levels of defensiveness. There may also be ways to combat the influx of Africanized drones from feral colonies. USDA researchers working in Costa Rica have developed drone bait traps that could prove effective in reducing the Africanized drone populations in specific areas. This might give the European bees a competitive edge in the mating game.

Thomas Rinderer says the mixing of genes in the coming years will probably create a wide variety of stable bee populations in the United States and that each will have some African characteristics and some European characteristics, with the dominant characteristics being determined, to some extent, by the environmental setting. Eventually, all the research questions about the impact of Africanization will be resolved by the bees themselves. Over many bee generations, but "within our lifetime," Rinderer says, the whole thing will get sorted out. Stay tuned.

CHAPTER SEVEN

Bees on Wheels

JUST AFTER MIDNIGHT, ON MAY 23, 1992, JOHN PAUL Shane was tooling down U.S. Highway 27 in northern Florida, accompanied by about five million honey bees safely enclosed in 250 hive boxes on the flat bed of his truck, when suddenly a car veered in front of him. Shane collided head-on with the vehicle and his rig tipped over. Injured and trapped inside the cab, he soon began to hear, see, and feel something that was even more terrifying than the accident itself. The bees were pouring out into the night air, and they were not happy.

"It was a nightmare," he told reporters later. "I was trapped for three hours underneath that load of bees and they were coming in where the windshield was supposed to be. I had diesel fuel running over me, and I didn't know whether I was going to burn up in a fire or get stung to death."

Firemen and rescue workers who arrived on the scene also came under attack from the furious bees and were initially forced back. Eventually, firemen soaked the bees with water from their high-pressure hoses and killed them. A front end loader from the Florida Department of Transportation had to be brought in to scoop the piles of dead bees off the asphalt.

Shane and four rescue workers were treated for multiple stings at a local hospital. The driver of the other vehicle was killed in the crash.

Shane had been taking the bees up the highway to pollinate agricultural crops on behalf of his employer, Horace Bell of Deland, Florida, who runs one of the biggest beekeeping operations in the United States. Mr. Bell is what is known as a migratory beekeeper, a man who moves his colonies to produce a better honey crop or to collect fees for pollinating crops. They often move north in the spring and summer to pollinate crops and then back south in the winter to keep the stock in good condition for the next year. There are only about a thousand migratory beekeepers in the United States, but their value to the nation's agriculture goes far beyond their numbers.

According to Roger Morse, 80 percent of all insect pollination in the United States is done by honey bees. Much of the high-intensity agriculture we rely on to produce the foods we like to eat, at prices we can afford, depends on getting those little buzzing fur balls into the fields at the right time. The use of pesticides over the years has reduced the number of feral bee colonies in some parts of the country, and even where there are wild bees, they are not always drawn right to the field the farmer wants pollinated.

Managed honey bee colonies can be trucked right into the middle of a field and set up according to the pollination needs of the customer. For some crops, one colony per acre is sufficient; for others it may take two or more. They sometimes use five colonies per acre to pollinate California almonds, the single biggest crop serviced by beekeepers who rent their hives for pollination. Alfalfa seed crops may require as many as ten. In all, about two million colonies of bees get trucked around on the roads each year to do pollination. Although the farmer often pays for this service, sometimes it is a proposition of mutual convenience, whereby the beekeeper gets a good honey crop and the farmer gets his field pollinated.

The life of the migratory beekeeper is a life closely connected with the life of the colony, and it is also a life on the road, moving

Honey bee colonies being unloaded for safflower pollination. Photo courtesy Kenneth Lorenzen, Department of Entomology, University of California, Davis

bees from Florida or Texas to the fields of the upper midwest in the summer, and then back south for the winter. There are also many migratory operators who do the run between California, where they pollinate fruit and nut crops, and the Dakotas, where summer provides an abundance of sweet clover, sunflowers, and other plants that produce good honey and, sometimes, good profits. Many operations stay right in California, where about two thirds of the nation's total annual pollination rentals take place.

In his wonderful book on migratory beekeepers, *Following the Bloom*, Douglas Whynott refers to them as "entomological cowboys," who haul bees over the range just as cowpokes from Texas used to drive cattle up north over the Chisholm trail. The migratory beemen sometimes face trouble, just as the old-time cowboys did. At times, gas station attendants turn them away for fear of getting stung. Now and then, restaurant owners refuse to let them park their trucks nearby while they get a bite to eat and, sometimes, people even threaten them with guns, telling them to "get them things outta here!"

Bee colonies stacked on semi-trailers generally represent little danger to anyone. They are well-secured and are removed only when the truck has reached its destination, which is usually a field somewhere far from town. But, on those rare occasions when something goes wrong, as it did for John Paul Shane, the public becomes aware of this practice and questions are raised about the safety of transporting bees over the roadways. As the Africanized honey bees make their way farther into the United States, concern has grown over what impact they could have on migratory operations. The bees involved in the Florida accident were normal European honey bees. What if there had been some Africanized hives in there? What if a truck full of Africanized bees were to tip over near a shopping center, or a school yard full of children? Imagine the pandemonium and the outcry. Imagine the honey flow for all the lawyers.

To avoid problems with the public, and to protect their colonies, some migratory beekeepers have used refrigerated trucks, which maintain the bees at a cool and calm 50 degrees Fahrenheit and keep them enclosed and inconspicuous. There is a danger of bees getting too chilled, however, and such trucks are obviously more expensive to buy and operate.

Perhaps the biggest problem the Africanized bee will present for the migratory bee-pokes, other than the public safety problem, will be the general orneriness and difficulty for which they are famous. Many experts doubt that Africanized bees will stand for being lifted in their hive boxes in and out of trucks and trundled about in fields. These bees have a tendency to leave and never come back when conditions are not to their liking.

The other problem for migratory beekeeping is that Africanized bees might be given a "lift" into uninfested areas by infiltrating the beekeeper's colonies. To deal with this danger, authorities imposed a two-mile-radius quarantine around Hidalgo, Texas, after finding the first swarm of Africanized bees there in October of 1990. The quarantine was later extended to several other counties after additional swarms were discovered. Migratory beekeepers from up north who found themselves in those areas at that time were prevented from moving their colonies out until they had been inspected and certified as free of Africanization.

As the threat of Africanized bees grows, more and more states are developing management plans that are based on the USDA's model certification plan, which calls for inspection and certification of colonies in areas where the Africanized bees have been discovered. The relatively quick FABIS test can be used for this, but, depending on how bad the Africanized bee problem gets, delays and bureaucratic procedures could become a big headache for the migratory bee jockeys.

Experts say the danger of a professional migratory bee operation carrying African-tainted colonies across state lines is actually minimal since they are the biggest and most visible beekeepers and, therefore, the ones the apiary inspectors are going to spend the most time checking out. The migratory beekeepers are also interested in protecting themselves and will be vigilant with their own stock. Of more concern, some officials say, is that smaller-scale operators will move bees without even realizing the problems they could create. A guy could leave southern Texas with a pickup truck full of colonies he wants to set up on his brother's farm up in Nebraska. A farmer who keeps some bees behind the barn could pass away, leaving his property, his equipment, and his bees to family members from various other states who divide it up and truck it on out. No state has enough inspectors to check all the vehicles travelling in and out, so there are bound to be gaping holes in every well-intentioned system of control.

Of course, quarantines and restrictions on bee colony movements are not new. There have already been regulations established to deal with two invading mites that infest bees and which, at this point, probably threaten the beekeeping industry in the United States far more than do the Africanized bees. The tracheal mite, which appeared in 1984, is a microscopic little animal that gets into the breathing tubes of honey bees. The *Varroa* mite, which came along a couple of years later, is larger and is mainly harmful because it feeds on developing bee larvae.

An even greater danger for U.S. agriculture would be an exaggerated public response to severe stinging incidents involving the Africanized bees, even if they have nothing to do with migratory beekeepers. Politicians might rise up to defend the public by placing restrictions on inter-state operations, thereby reducing the number of bee colonies available to farmers, and, in the end, reducing the crop yields. A 1984 USDA study showed that just a one percent decline in production of the vegetables, fruits, and nuts that rely on bee pollination would reduce American consumer welfare by about $87 million, and this does not include the high food prices that would result from reduced production of bee-pollinated seed crops. An over-reaction to the perceived threat of "killer bees" invading the heartland could actually end up putting a real crimp in our cornucopia.

Early Arrivals

When speaking of the Africanized bees found in Texas in 1990, we say that they were the first to cross "overland" into the United States, or that they were the first bees found from the "migrating front." We would be incorrect in saying that they were the first Africanized bees, or for that matter, African bees, to have entered the United States. Beekeepers are always experimenting with different varieties of bees and back in the 19th century, there were bee enthusiasts who travelled to the Middle East, Asia and Africa to find bees that would be good producers. They brought some of these back to the United States and, no doubt, many of the bees we call "European" in our nation today are actually a veritable potpourri of various genetic strains of *Apis mellifera*.

Even though there are now tight restrictions on the import of bees into the United States, there is no way of maintaining 100 percent control. Practically every day, illegal shipments of cocaine and heroin enter the United States, in spite of a massive law enforcement effort aimed at stopping the flow of drugs. There are, no doubt, some unscrupulous beekeepers who have smuggled in African queens just for fun or profit. But the impact of such activity is probably trivial when compared to the swarms of Africanized bees that have come to U.S. ports over the years on board ships coming from Latin American destinations. Routine harbor inspections have led to the disposal of more than 20 Africanized swarms on ships in the past decade, but there have also been times when ship crewmen said something like, "Oh yeah, we had this swarm of bees up in one of the cargo areas, but they disappeared about the time we came close to land."

The most famous incident involving Africanized bees in the United States before their overland arrival occurred near Lost Hills, California, in the summer of 1985, when the operator of an earthmover saw some bees furiously attacking a rabbit. Protected inside his cab, he buried the colony and later reported it to authorities, who inspected the colony and found it to be Africanized. This prompted a huge quarantine effort, covering more than 3,000 square miles. A task force assembled and checked apiaries and wild nesting sites all over the quarantine zone. The state and national media had a field day, churning out alarmist "killer bee" stories. By early December, more than one million dollars had been spent, 22,000 colonies had been inspected, some beekeepers had their colonies destroyed by the state and had gotten fined on top of it, and a total of 12 confirmed Africanized colonies had been discovered and eradicated.

The Africanized bees that entered California probably came into a port on board a ship from South America, but no one knows for sure when they arrived. They could have been out there in the wild, mixing with both feral and apiary bees for a year or two before being discovered. The public reaction they produced provides a possible preview for what will happen once these fierce bees settle into an urban area and start doing some serious stinging.

Semen to Beemen

Another way that Africanized bees may have mixed in with U.S. bees long before the arrival of the overland swarms was through a breeding experiment conducted in 1961 at the USDA-ARS Bee Research Laboratory in Baton Rouge. Researcher Steve Taber collected bee semen from various parts of the world, which he used to artificially inseminate queens in the lab's experimental apiary. Among the contributors to his little experiment was a Brazilian fellow named Warwick Kerr, who sent Taber several shipments of Africanized bee semen.

Taber says he used the semen to produce queens and colonies which were "over 90 percent *Apis mellifera scutellata*." When the stories of stinging incidents in Brazil reached the United States, the USDA ordered all of Taber's stock destroyed, but the story did not die there. Many beekeepers around the United States persist in the belief that the government somehow screwed up in this experiment and introduced at least some Africanization into apiaries in the Baton Rouge area.

Some of these beekeepers would put the best political conspiracy hacks to shame, but there is at least one of them who has a plausible story that lacks any indication of exaggeration. His name is Richard Adee. He is the president of the American Honey Producers and he is a big-scale migratory beekeeper. In fact, he probably operates the single biggest private beekeeping operation in the world. Adee lives in Bruce, South Dakota, where he has a tiny office attached to his warehouse on the main street, which is just about the only street in the small town. From Bruce, Adee sends out semitrailer loads of bee colonies to take advantage of blooming plants in other parts of the Midwest and in the South. For the most part, he is not a beekeeper who rents colonies for pollination; he is interested in producing prodigious amounts of honey for sale. Richard Adee has more than 40,000 colonies of honey bees, which produce about four and half million pounds of honey each year. He has a queen-breeding operation in Mississippi and has overwintered as many as

30,000 colonies at a location just up the river from Baton Rouge.

In the early 1970s Adee and his workers began having some problems with some of their colonies. They were swarming a lot and showing increased aggressiveness. He spoke with another bee-keeper he knew down in Louisiana, named Billy Bassinet, who was having an even worse time with his bees. They concluded that African strains that had mixed into the feral bee population around Baton Rouge must have infiltrated their colonies.

Adee says he was able to requeen and dilute the African influence out of his bees eventually and that Bassinet sold his fiery bees to another beekeeper who trucked them back up to his home in Missouri. Adee says the Missouri beekeeper had "never in his life seen such mean bees." He requeened all the colonies, and that took care of the problem. In spite of all this, Adee has a philosophical atti-tude about the use of the African bee semen in the USDA research.

"It was a legitimate experiment," he says. "I guess we can't blame them too much because (at the time) they were not aware of some of the African bee's undesirable characteristics, otherwise they would not have brought them in, in the first place."

For his part, Steve Taber, who has retired from USDA and now lives in France, says that Adee "...has a bit of an imagination, but on the other hand, most beekeepers do anyway."

As to whether the introduction of the Africanized bee semen could have started a wave of Africanization here in the United States just as the introduction of the African queens did in Brazil, Thomas Rinderer, for one, does not think so. He says such a small popula-tion would create an "in-bred line" which would not survive long. He says samples taken from honey bee colonies, both wild and managed, all over Louisiana, have shown no sign of African geno-type influence. He believes the story of Taber's African bees has taken on the character of beekeeper folklore, whereby some bee-keepers think that any colony that starts getting a little testy must have African genes that can be traced back to Taber's study.

Rinderer says that any introduction of Africanized bees into the United States that consists of only a small population, such as a swarm or two escaping from a ship, or from an experimental apiary, will quickly die out in the wild, or be diluted out of existence through contact with European bees.

"What is important here is the concept of critical mass," says Rinderer. "The occasional swarm is not going to be doing very much mating with itself, so you will have a hybrid formed, if it does produce any progeny. They will have to mate with European bees, so you are going to have a dilution very quickly from a single swarm."

Rinderer says an example that illustrates the concept comes from the introduction of a European bird, the starling, into North America during the last century. Several attempts to establish the bird failed because too few birds had been brought in. Later, he says, a massive number were imported and the starling propagated to the point where it is a major pest today.

Along with most other experts, Rinderer believes the introduction of the African bee in Brazil got off the ground, not from 26 escaped swarms, but from the creation of critical mass through the distribution of hybrid queens.

"The Brazilians brought in a good number and then they propagated them. They reared queens and sent them off to beekeepers and then, unfortunately, the second year, they reared queens and sent them off again, which meant that you had African-by-African matings. They really concentrated the stuff and got it off the ground with large numbers of bees."

Is a critical mass of Africanized bees now building in south Texas? Perhaps. If so, the maintenance of a healthy beekeeping industry in that area is going to be the nation's most important line of defense. Regulations on migratory beekeepers operating there may cause some headaches and delays now and then, but most beekeepers seem willing to go along with these measures in the hope that no stronger actions will ever be necessary.

Bees in the Beekeeper's Bonnet

As the Africanized bees move farther into Texas, the reaction from beekeepers around the country runs from irritation over news media reports that could stir up public fear of bees in general to alarm over what the Africanized invasion could mean for an industry that is already beleaguered with two mites and a variety of bee diseases. Adding to

Photo above: Suiting up for the AHB.
Photo courtesy Jerrold Summerlin, Texas Agricultural Extension Service

beekeeper headaches is a looming political threat. Concern over the US deficit has focused attention on the honey price support system which is designed to protect the US beekeeping industry from cheap foreign imports of honey and to maintain a healthy bee population in the United States to perform vital pollination services. Some politicians, however, view the price support program as a pork barrel scheme that lines the pockets of a few big beekeepers at the expense of the taxpayer and consumer. Beekeepers have had a hard time explaining their importance to agriculture and have found that the prevailing attitude in some sectors is that bees will pollinate plants whether there is a subsidy for beekeepers or not.

In the face of all this, many beekeepers have grown testy about the whole subject of Africanized bees. What many of them fear most is a public reaction to the threat of "killer bees" which could lead to higher insurance costs, restrictive legislation, and limited access to fields of flowering plants. Texas officials say some land owners who had previously allowed beekeepers to keep colonies on their property are now turning them away out of fear of the "killer bees."

Beekeeper attitudes tend to split along the line that separates the more than 200,000 small-time and hobbyist beekeepers from the 5,000 or so operators who, together, produce more than 90 percent of the U.S. honey crop and carry out almost all of the pollination services.

Most experts believe the hobbyist beekeepers will be the first to go when the Africanized bees arrive in any given place. No one will be able to keep bees anywhere near a populated area once the aggressive bees take over. Hobbyists would probably not be able to afford the insurance they would need to buy, nor would most of them be able to afford the additional equipment, the cost of requeening, and other expenses that would come with the invading bees. Managing bees who are prone to abscond and swarm frequently will also be beyond the capabilities of many hobbyists. Some hobbyists see the Africanized bee as a threat to a great American rural tradition and look to the government for more help. Larger operators, however, fear over-regulation more than the Africanized bees. Some of them sniff with indignation when talking about the small timers. As one puts it, "You don't call everyone who has a garden a farmer, yet everyone who has a hive of bees gets called a beekeeper."

Big beekeepers are also more confident about their ability to cope. Richard Adee, for example, went on a USDA-sponsored trip to visit apiaries in Mexico and Central America in 1991, and he says, "we never found any bees we could not handle." Adee recognizes the difficulties the African progeny will present, but he does not believe these bees will create a crisis for the beekeeping industry.

Fellow South Dakotan Don Schmidt, on the other hand, says he thinks Adee and some of the other big operators may be viewing the problem "through rose-colored glasses." Schmidt, who maintains colonies for honey production at a permanent location near Winner, South Dakota, also worries about migratory beekeepers bringing Africanized bees into areas where they do not yet exist and how that might effect beekeepers who do not move their stock.

Both of these gentlemen from South Dakota head separate national beekeeping organizations, which also tend to take slightly different positions at times on various beekeeping issues. Adee is president of the American Honey

Producers and Schmidt is president of the American Beekeeping Federation. In the face of the political threat to the honey subsidy and possible public over-reaction to the Africanized bee invasion, both organizations have worked to educate the public on the importance of bees and beekeepers to American agriculture.

The Bee Buster of Bellaire

The way Houston area beekeeper Darrell Lister sees it, there will be hell to pay once the Africanized bees start building up big populations in urban areas and he has sounded warning bells about the danger they represent. As a result, he is regarded by some people as an "extremist" who could provoke an unwarranted panic. He has clashed with many of his fellow beekeepers over the issue. They tried to drive him out of the local beekeeping association and at least one man threatened his life.

Lister is known in Houston as the "Bee Buster," because of the bee colony removal service he operates out of his home in the suburb of Bellaire. During the months when swarms of bees invade suburban yards and homes, he makes between $50,000 and $70,000 a season removing the pests from homes and apartment buildings. In addition, The "Bee Buster" of Bellaire has developed a slide show presentation on the Africanized bees based on experiences he and his wife, Carolyn, have had while travelling in South and Central America to get a first-hand look at the problem. On their trips they have often spoken with family members of people who died in Africanized bee attacks.

His detractors say Lister is stirring up public worries over the bee invasion as a way of improving business for himself, but he says his main concern is to raise public awareness and to protect people from possibly tragic encounters with the fierce bees. He has advocated more of a role in bee removal for fire departments, using the basic approach that Latin American nations have developed. But the Texas legislature has ruled out bee removal by anyone other than a licensed pest controller, unless there is an emergency situation. If a beekeeper, with years of experience in handling swarm removal, wants to get a license, he or she has to pay around $100 in fees, pass a lengthy exam and buy liability insurance that will cost several hundred dollars more. In order to keep going as the "Bee Buster," Darrell Lister got his license, but he still thinks police and fire departments should be at the front in the battle with the bees.

"They say, if you let the fire department do your business, then you are going to lose money," Lister says. "Yeah, but it is more important for the public to be served than it is for me to make a little bit of money."

Lister says the fire department could respond more quickly than pest controllers to remove swarms in open areas, before they invade someone's house, where the potential for a severe stinging attack on a family would be much greater. The other problem with bees getting into buildings, according to Lister, is that the residue they leave keeps them coming back.

"Once that honey bee is established there and that honey is in the wall, it is very difficult to keep that building from being marked," he says. For this reason, he always goes in between walls, if necessary, to remove comb, honey residue and pheromone odors that could attract another swarm. Lister says some pest control companies are going to make money off the Africanized bees by charging to remove bees and then charging again to remove subsequent swarms that come to the same place.

The "Bee Buster" says Houston will provide an inviting home for the Africanized bees. One example he points to are large forested areas around the International Airport, which will provide shelter for swarms who can then build up numbers and move into nearby suburban residential areas. Lister says he is going to quit his own beekeeping once the Africanized bees arrive in force and he worries that the problem will not be fully addressed by public officials until "somebody gets killed."

The Top Texas Beeman

The man who has been on the bee frontlines for more than ten years in Texas is John Thomas, who in 1992 retired as chief entomologist at Texas A & M University but who remains active with the university's extension service and with the state beekeeping association. Although he disagrees with Darrell Lister on the degree of danger to public health the bees will create, he agrees with the "Bee Buster" on one point: that the invading critters are more likely to kick up a fuss in populated areas of the state than in rural areas.

"Bees have three requirements," says Thomas, "a nest, food, and water. All three are far more abundant in Houston or San Antonio than they are out in the country."

Thomas notes that bees invading suburban parks and woodlots have "plants from around the world" to exploit in both small backyard gardens and in large landscaped areas. He says houses in residential zones will offer potential nest sites that are protected from the elements. In rural areas, by contrast, Thomas says modern agricultural methods have eliminated some of the variety of foraging opportunities and left fewer ideal nesting sites.

The bees are also more likely to create problems in urban areas, according to Thomas, because that's where the people are. "In rural areas," he says, "people see a nest of bees and leave them alone, there is no need to call a removal service," whereas in urban areas the potential for contact is greater since there are more people living in closer proximity.

Thomas says the urban areas can be protected through abatement programs to eliminate wild swarms. He says bees normally do not establish more than four or five colonies per square mile, since the food resources in an area that size generally cannot support more than that. He favors a change in current rulings of the Texas State Structural Pest Control Board that would allow easier certification of police officers, fire fighters, and beekeepers for the specific task of bee nest removal. Thomas, who has kept bee colonies since 1942 and confesses to a love for "bugs" says beekeepers, in particular, are going to be the most important line of defense against the Africanized bees, both because of the genetic dilution they can promote by maintaining European colonies, and because of the experience they can bring to controlling what otherwise might turn into a problem for the general public. "What the beekeepers bring to the table is a total knowledge of this animal," he says, "they know what it does, how to deal with it, and how to handle it."

CHAPTER EIGHT

"Fire Above, Fire Below!"

In Texas, as the old joke goes, "everything is big" and that includes the bug population. There are some 37,000 species of insects in Texas, more than in any other single state. This is due to the wide variety of terrain and the abundant rainfall in many areas. Lately, however, some Texans have begun to wonder just what it is they have done to deserve such insect abundance. If it isn't one variety of bug biting the flesh, then it's another chomping on the rose bushes or the cotton crop. Crawling and buzzing critters seem right at home "deep in the heart of Texas."

As the Africanized bees were entering Texas, about half of the Lone Star state had already been occupied by another "stinging sensation," which had also come from South America, the imported fire ant. The forward lines of the two invaders met somewhere in southern Texas in 1991. At that point, it was not clear what impact the bees would have, but the people of eastern Texas already knew, from hard experience, what to expect from the fire ants.

Texas A & M entomologist John Thomas laments the effect the fiery invaders have had on areas near his home. "The fire ant has changed the way we enjoy the outdoors," he says. "Even the simplest act, like changing a tire on the side of the road has to be viewed with caution because fire ants are everywhere."

The ants making life miserable for millions of people in Texas and other parts of the South are called "imported," although no one deliberately brought them into the United States. They are similar to the Africanized bees, in that their spread has been aided by humans, unintentionally. There are two species that came from South America, the black fire ant, *Solenopsis richteri*, which is native to Uruguay, Paraguay, southern Brazil and northern Argentina, and the red fire ant, *Solenopsis invicta*, which is mainly found in tropical forest areas from northern Argentina to central Brazil. The first invasion, that of the black ants, came around 1918 when, it is believed, ships carrying cargo from South America docked in Mobile, Alabama, and the ants came ashore. From Mobile, they moved into other areas of the South and today are found mainly in northern Mississippi and Alabama. The red ants came later, probably in the late 1930s, and by the 1960s had spread to the easternmost part of Texas and to parts of Florida, Georgia and the Carolinas. They displaced the less numerous and less toxic native fire ants and spread like wildfire. *Solenopsis invicta* now covers more than 260 million acres in 11 southern states, including at least half of Texas, and its slow but steady march continues.

Wherever they have appeared, the imported red fire ants have made a strong impression. One or two stings can send an upright citizen into a frenzy of jumping, screaming and removing of clothing in public. Anyone who inadvertently steps on a mound will soon find an army of angry little guys marching up the leg, stitching a pattern of burning stings along the way. No one who has suffered a sting needs an explanation as to why they are called fire ants. The toxin produces a burning sore that often develops into a white pustule. Fire ants sting up to five million people in the United States each year, about one percent of whom develop an allergic reaction. In rare cases, the reaction has been fatal.

The imported fire ants have also caused damage to agriculture by covering pastures and fields with their mounds, each measuring as high as a foot and half. Some types of harvesting machinery have come out the worse after an encounter with these mounds. The imported fire ants have eaten buds and developing fruit from plants, devastating crops of berries, beans, okra and citrus. They have ravaged whole fields of sorghum. The ants have even attacked small animals, in the wild and on farms. There have been reports of young calves being killed by fire ants and of some animals being blinded when the ants crawled up to feast on the mucus around the eyes.

But the fire ants have not been confined to rural zones. They have also disrupted the quality of life in more populated areas by invading city parks and suburban lawns. Picnics have become an impossibility in some areas. Children's playgrounds have been abandoned and people have shunned their favorite fishing holes because sitting on a grassy bank has become risky. The fire ants have even gotten into electrical equipment, causing short circuits and power outages. A few years ago, entomologists at Texas A & M discovered that the ants were drawn to relay switches by the electrical fields they produce. Why they respond to the fields is still unclear but at least a solution to the problem can be found in sealing off relay switches and putting insecticides around traffic light control consoles, airport runway lights, air conditioner units and other outdoor electrical equipment boxes.

But all the research and all the millions of dollars spent on prevention and control have had very little impact on the fire ant problem. Today, people accept them. They may hate them, but they accept them. Politicians may try to "fire up" their campaigns with promises to do something about the menace, but the officials working on control programs realize that there is not much that can be done.

Bart Drees, a Texas Agriculture official who has worked on both the fire ant problem and the Africanized bee invasion sees some similarities between the two and he believes both problems need to be faced with sustained programs that include public education components along with control measures. As is the case with the Africanized bees, Drees says, much lies in the perception of the problem. Someone who has had a very bad, direct experience with either pest will perceive the threat as bigger than will the average person who has had minimal contact with the invaders. Farmers whose fields are full of ant mounds and whose crops have been eaten up will see *Solenopsis invicta* as "the ant from hell." Farmers who have been able to adapt will see it as just another irritating obstacle to overcome. As we have already seen, beekeepers have divided along similar lines in their reaction to the Africanized honey bee.

While acknowledging that more study needs to be done, Bart Drees says the overall costs to agriculture and apiculture from the two insect invasions is probably not significant. He sees the impact of both as mainly a social and medical problem, in that people are restricted in their enjoyment of the outdoors and, if stung, could suffer a severe reaction. The general public, he says, will be more affected by the fire ant, but the potential for serious injury or death may be greater with the Africanized bee, since allergic reactions to bee venom are far more common than reactions to ant stings, and because there is an increased likelihood of massive bee stinging incidents now that the Africanized bees are here.

Once a few spectacular "killer bee" attacks hit the newspaper headlines, the call for a magic bullet solution to a complicated natural problem is likely to rise again. The experience with fire ants provides a preview. Decades after their arrival in Texas, Bart Drees says, there are people who still look for a complete eradication of the scourge. But Drees and other officials, both state and federal, have come to understand that finding such a solution is not only unlikely; it may even be undesirable.

In the 1950s, USDA officials declared war on *Solenopsis invicta*, spraying a pesticide called heptachlor over 27 million acres of southern crop land. The program succeeded in killing a lot of fire ants but the majority just hunkered down in their mounds like soldiers waiting out an air raid. The USDA kept trying until 1962, when

Rachel Carson wrote her now famous book, *Silent Spring*, in which she criticized such massive use of pesticides for the effect it was having on birds, fish and other animals who were not the targets, but who suffered the consequences. An effort was then made to find other pesticides that would not harm wildlife but which would still be effective against the ants. Environmentalists, however, soon found harmful effects on animals and humans resulting from these chemicals as well. The worst result of the USDA spraying programs was that more than 20 years and $170 million after they began, the imported red fire ants remained and, if anything, seemed stronger than ever. To add insult to injury, researchers found that the pesticides had actually helped *Solenopsis invicta* to continue its offensive by killing many of the insects and other predators who prey on fire ant queens.

Researchers now look to methods of controlling the ants right up close, mound by mound. This is not easy, however, since the ants are quite resilient. Just when a colony seems deader than a doornail, signs of life appear again and, as they say in the horror movies — "They're back!" Even experts are often baffled by the survivability of the fire ants. Preston Sides, the director of the Harris County, Texas, agricultural extension office says he sometimes wonders if the little buggers don't come back from the dead. Agriculture officials in Texas have been besieged, not only by farmers, but by gardeners, outdoorsmen and suburbanites with lawns to defend — all desperate for a cure that isn't available. With the advance of the Africanized bees, many people worry if it will ever again be safe to go outdoors. Sides finds himself, once again, with little comfort to offer. "You may end up getting stung on the ear by one and on the foot by the other, " he says. "All you can do is hop and slap."

But Sides and other agriculture officials, in Texas and elsewhere, have also tried to promote public education as a way of giving people a realistic approach to the problem. While the suggestion to study about life in the ant nest or bee colony may not appeal much to someone who has just been stung, it can sometimes help people from being attacked. Knowing more about the fascinating life of social insects like ants and bees can also bring a psychological benefit, reducing the irrational fear of these creatures that can sometimes make reactions to stinging incidents worse than they should be. Understanding the biology of these insect invaders can also provide a better idea of how to control them.

In the case of fire ants, for example, entomologists know that they often come back after appearing to have been wiped out because chemicals applied directly to the mounds usually have only a superficial effect. Each of those mounds is built like Saddam Hussein's bunker. They contain a labyrinth of tunnels and chambers that can extend as far as six feet down into the earth, with horizontal foraging passages, just under the surface, extending out as far as 130 feet from the mound. Many pesticides affect only the uppermost passages, killing a few thousand of the hundreds of thousands of worker ants while others, deeper down, scurry about to move the queen to safety.

As is the case with bees, as long as there is a queen, the colony can survive. Ants and honey bees are both social insects and, while there are some big differences between them, there are also some striking similarities. The ant queen, for example, sprouts wings and goes on a "nuptial flight" several hundred feet up in the air, just as the queen bee does. She also engages in "killer sex" with the winged males going out in a blaze of glory as they deposit their sperm, just as the bee drones do. After returning to earth, the queens shed their wings and try to dig in to the earth. All but a very few perish along the way, mostly from predators, which include birds, armadillos and even other ants. Once the queen gets dug in and starts laying eggs (at the rate of up to 200 a day), it takes several months to produce a conspicuous surface mound. Once a full colony is established, however, it can contain up to 500,000 workers and up to several hundred winged varieties.

In the 1970s, southerners began discovering huge, inter-connected, multiple queen colonies of imported red fire ants. Prior to this, it had been believed that all colonies contained a single queen and that colonies competed with each other. Multiple queen colonies have now been found in Florida, Louisiana, Mississippi, Georgia, and Texas. One enormous colony found in Mississippi contained more than 3,000 queens! In the multiple queen colonies, workers move freely from one mound to another, resulting in a ten-fold increase in the number of mounds per acre. A farmer who has single queen fire ant colonies, for example, may have 40 to 150 mounds per acre, whereas the poor fellow plagued with multiple queen colonies may have anywhere from 200 to 800 mounds per acre.

Since the widespread use of chemical sprays has been abandoned, experts now recommend two basic treatments to control fire ants. The most common approach is the attack on individual mounds with such weapons as chemical drenches, surface dusts, injected toxins, fumigants, and certain biological deterrents, including nematodes and mites that attack the ants and their larvae. Some electrical and mechanical cures have been marketed but their effectiveness is questionable. The other approach is to broadcast poisoned bait in the area where there are mounds. There are obvious problems with all these methods, ranging from limited effectiveness to potential environmental damage. There is also the cost. Since re-infestation will occur within six months or so even with the most effective treatments, the effort and expense must be repeated endlessly.

But while management of the fire ant problem may be difficult, it can be done, and many farmers have found ways of adapting to the inevitable presence of the ants. For example, they have found that switching from square bales of hay to round bales reduces the risk of ant attacks on field workers. They have also minimized damage to harvesting equipment by converting from sickle bar harvesters to disc cutters in some areas. What's more, some farmers see the imported red fire ants as beneficial. They eat boll weevils in cotton fields and prey on ticks and flies in pasture lands. *Solenopsis invicta* is also known to dine on sugarcane borer and corn ear worms. Many people will be happy to learn that they also snack on cockroaches and their eggs. So, judgment of even the dreaded fire ant depends on point of view.

Whether seen as beneficial or not, experts agree that both the imported fire ant and the Africanized honey bee are here to stay, at least in parts of the South. The bees may eventually find a northern climatic limit and the fire ants appear to have trouble moving into the drier, western areas. Control efforts should limit both insects' negative impact on human society to some extent, but humans in the effected areas are also going to have to take them into account whenever they plan outdoor activities. Just as rattlesnakes can crawl onto a suburban lawn and pose a threat, bees can nest in the bushes or in the backyard shed, and fire ants can build their extensive bunkers under the grass. The beleaguered suburbanite can only take precautions, implement control measures, and be prepared to deal with incidents as they occur.

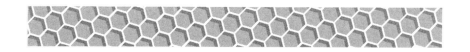

CHAPTER NINE

Bee Safe

WHETHER THE AFRICANIZED BEES TURN OUT TO BE A MINOR threat or a major problem in the United States, there is no question that some individuals are going to experience the pain, and perhaps even the tragedy, of an encounter with the testy little critters. People whose idea of an outing is to go from the house to the air-conditioned car and then to the artificial environment of a shopping mall will have little opportunity to meet the "killer bees." However, those who like to hunt and fish, bicycle, canoe, hike, climb rocks, and in any other way enjoy the great outdoors just might. Likewise, there could be a threat for people who need to work outside — farmers, construction workers, park rangers, lawn and garden service people, and even pest control agents.

In the previous chapters, you learned about the bees themselves and why they attack, you learned about what happened to some people who were attacked, and you learned how beekeepers in some places have learned to work with them. But safety depends on more than knowing about the bees, it depends on knowing what to do long before the moment of crisis comes.

Bee Alert

The most important thing to know is how to avoid an encounter. If you live in an area that has already been invaded by the Africanized bees, then you should stay vigilant. Check around your house and yard to see if there are any signs of bees taking up residence. If you do find a colony, leave it alone and keep your family and pets away. Call a pest control company or a local beekeeper to deal with the bees. If your local community has developed a special office or designated an already existing body (i.e. the fire department, pest control board, or agricultural extension office) as the proper authority to deal with bee colonies, then you should call them. If your community does not have any plan in place, you might want to petition local authorities to develop one and to provide proper training for the persons designated to respond to bee complaints. They might avail themselves of training in such control methods as the soapy water procedure, whereby the bees are given a bath to end all baths.

Research has found that a one per cent solution of dishwashing detergent or some other similar chemical agent will immobilize honey bees and kill them within 60 seconds. However, you should not attempt to douse a colony of wild bees you happen to find in your backyard unless you have had proper training and are wearing protective clothing. It is best to leave such operations to the local fire department, since the personnel there already have protective suits and only need to acquire veils to be fully prepared for battle with bees. Fire departments also have high pressure hoses and foaming agents for controlling fires, which also work well in fending off angry bees. If you live in an area where Africanized bees are, or could soon become, a menace, make sure your local authorities have prepared firefighters, police, or some other agency or group to deal with bee situations.

When you are outdoors, in a rural area, a park or wilderness reserve, be aware of your surroundings and keep an eye out for bees

Educational poster distributed by Texas Agricultural Extension Service

the way you would watch out for snakes and other natural dangers. But do not panic at the sight of a bee foraging in the flowers. Bees are generally very docile as they go about their work and unless you do something really outrageous, such as step on them, they will not bother you. A bee can get entangled in hair or clothing, and when this happens, take care to help her escape. If she stings, she will release a pheromone that could attract other bees. Bees who have swarmed and landed on a tree or rock may be quite impressive, but they are unlikely to even notice you if you leave them alone. Since they have no nest to defend, swarms usually do not attack. However, as was mentioned previously, only experienced beekeepers should approach a swarm.

Obviously, it is best to avoid contact with any wild nest of insects, especially if they are bees or wasps, who have the advantage of flight. Many cases of Africanized bee attacks have been traced back to some provocation, such as a kid tossing a stone at the hive, or some noise or vibration, such as that of a lawnmower or tractor. Sometimes, however, people come under attack who have no idea what they have done to upset the bees. In some cases, they haven't done anything. Once disturbed by something, Africanized bees can range quite far from the source of irritation, attacking anything that looks threatening. Quite often bees will display some preliminary defensive behavior before going into a full-fledged attack. They may fly at your face or buzz around over your head. These signs should be heeded, since the bees may be telling you that you have come into their area and are too close to their colony for comfort — their comfort.

Bee Attack!

Once bees get riled up, the most important thing to do is get away as fast as possible. Do not try to retrieve belongings nearby. Do not try to stand still in an attempt to fool the bees — that may work with a snake, under certain circumstances, but bees won't be impressed. Do not try to fight the bees — they have the advantage of numbers and the gift of flight. The more you flail your arms, the madder they will get. A bee can attain speeds of from 12 to 15 miles per hour, but most healthy humans can outrun them. So, run, and when you run — keep running. Africanized bees have been known to follow people for more than a mile!

Any covering for your body, and especially for your head and face will help you escape. While outdoor enthusiasts can hardly be expected to go around in bee suits, a small mosquito net device that fits over the head could easily be carried in a pocket. People who have been attacked say the worst part is having the darned things going into your face and stinging your eyes. Any impairment of your vision will also make it more difficult to escape. So, even though a net over your head may leave the rest of your body exposed, it will allow you to see where you are going as you run for your life.

If you happen not to have your net with you, grab a blanket, a coat, anything that will give you momentary relief while you look for an avenue of escape. But remember the story of Claudette Mo, in Chapter One. She used a cover but found the bees coming up under it. The covering device is not going to protect you for long. The idea is to use it to help you get away.

There is some disagreement about how to run from a bee attack. Some people say the important thing is speed. They recommend that you run as fast as possible in a straight line away from the scene of the attack. Most experts suggest that you run in a zig-zag pattern, in order to confuse the bees. Another suggestion is that you run through any brush or foliage that may be nearby. The reason for this is that bees do not see very well and have trouble navigating through branches and leaves. This may explain another incident mentioned in Chapter One — the one where the man fleeing on horseback was killed and the man who dove into the bushes survived.

Of course, there are going to be circumstances in which escape is not an option, or perhaps, less of an option. Elderly people and small children may not be able to outrun the bees. Everything depends on the exact circumstances, but a generally good idea is to cover such people quickly with a heavy blanket or tarp, of a light color, if possible. Experience has shown that bees like to attack dark things. Dark clothing, dark hair — anything dark in color could draw the bees. USDA's Ralph Iwamoto says that when he used to inspect apiaries he could often tell that they were Africanized by the number of stings he got in his black leather camera case!

A large white canvas tarp, like the ones painters use, might be a good thing to have along on excursions, just in case. If the bees are really worked up they will not leave a person alone, even if he or she is down on the ground and covered up. A covered person, however, will have a better chance than one who is not covered and the cover might buy them some time until help arrives.

Beekeepers commonly use smoke to control bees, but if you were under attack, you would need a lot of smoke in a hurry. Placing someone under a tarp near a smoky campfire might provide a bit more protection but if there is no fire already going, forget about trying to start one — the bees are unlikely to give you that much time! Another method that has been tested by USDA researchers is the use of a direct stream of insect repellant to hold back the attackers. Tests have shown that repellants containing DEET work best. Although the stuff will repel mosquitoes and most other insects when it is applied to skin and clothing, it does not seem to have much deterrent effect on angry bees. Only the direct aerosol stream slows them down. In Costa Rica and other parts of Latin America, bee removal teams generally use the soapy water technique to immobilize and kill feral colonies. They have found that it can also be useful in fending off attacks when sprayed directly at the bees. They do not recommend this to the general public, however, since it would be pretty hard to spray fast enough to hold off hundreds of angry bees, especially if you are not wearing any protective clothing. And, unless you happen to be washing dishes at the time the bees decide to attack, you probably won't have any soapy water readily available.

If possible, you should take refuge in a house, a tent, or a car with the windows and doors closed. If there is any opening, the bees will likely find it. Some bees are bound to enter with you, but you should be able to swat them easily enough, and even if you do get stung a few times, remember that each bee can only sting once. As long as the number inside the shelter with you is small, you have the advantage.

Ouch!

What about stings? The best thing to do is to scrape the sting out with a knife blade or with your fingernail. Remember that the bee's sting and poison sac tear out when she pulls away, so the venom can continue pumping even after the bee has gone. The sooner you get the barbed sting out of your flesh the better, but if you press down on the sac or squeeze it, you could cause more venom to flow out into your skin. After removing the sting, you can wash the area with water or swab it with alcohol. If there is swelling, you can apply ice, but do not be overly concerned. Local swelling is a normal reaction.

A sting in the eye can be especially painful and dangerous. Not only does the sting cause potential damage to the eye and its functioning, but a sting in this sensitive area can also produce some general body reactions. Consult a doctor as soon as possible if you get a sting to the eye or eye lid. Another danger is that bees sometimes enter the nostrils or go into the mouth of a victim. In one tragic case in Panama, a man who was attacked while fishing dove into the water. The bees hovered over the water for a long time, hitting him every time he came up for air. He died as a result of a bee getting into his throat and stinging him in the windpipe, which swelled shut so tight that doctors doing the autopsy found no water in his lungs.

How dangerous is the venom from stings? That depends. There have been people who survived hundreds of stings and there have been people who died from a relative few. There are, of course, other factors that could contribute to death in stinging incidents.

Some people have weak hearts that give out when they are terror-stricken. People running in panic from stinging insects sometimes stumble and injure themselves. But if all such incidental factors are set aside, bees and other stinging insects present two types of mortal danger to mammals — allergic reaction and mass envenomation from numerous stings.

Allergies to bee stings

A person with a severe allergy to the proteins found in bee venom could die from one sting, whether it be that of an Africanized or European bee. Anyone, whether allergic or not, can succumb to a large amount of venom entering their blood stream very quickly, as happens when someone suffers a massive number of stings. To complicate this a bit further, a person who has had no severe reaction to bee stings in the past can develop an allergic response if suddenly stung by a large number of bees.

So how can you know if you are allergic? What can you do if you are? First, let's examine what an allergy is and how reactions develop. An allergy is a tendency of the body to react to substances that are introduced from outside. Generally, these are proteins from plants or animals. Remember that bees collect pollen for the protein and that people with allergies to pollen sneeze when it is in the air. An allergic reaction comes after there has already been at least one contact with the foreign protein, known as the allergen. There is no noticeable reaction at the first contact although, within the body, there is a change known as sensitization which will produce adverse reactions to later contacts. The reactions we notice — sneezing, tissue swelling, and rashes — are produced by the release of histamine and other chemicals from the cells affected by the allergen.

Only one to two percent of the population has a clinical hypersensitivity to insect stings and, even among that small group, the risk of severe reaction is not considered great. People sometimes discover their allergy when the second sting they receive produces either a strong local, or a more general, systemic reaction. Local reactions include rashes and swelling, whereas systemic reactions can involve difficulty in breathing, fainting and loss of consciousness. Normal reaction to stings usually involves pain at the site, which lasts only a few minutes, and is then followed by some swelling and sometimes by wheals or other skin reactions near the site, which can remain for a day or two. These symptoms usually do not indicate hypersensitivity. More pronounced skin reactions can indicate a certain degree of sensitivity, but a physician should be consulted to determine if the symptoms indicate hypersensitivity. Only about 20 percent of the people having pronounced reactions to a second sting develop a severe, life-threatening hypersensitivity.

Most allergic reactions to insect stings in the United States are produced by bees, wasps, and fire ants. All are social insects and belong to the group *Hymenoptera*. The venoms they produce have similarities, but a person who is hypersensitive to one is not necessarily hypersensitive to another. While fire ant stings have been known to produce some fatal cases of anaphylactic shock, most insect sting fatalities in the United States are produced by bees and wasps, with honey bees and yellowjackets apparently being the worst offenders. The "apparently" is added because many victims have trouble telling whether the insect that stung them was a honey bee, a bumble bee, a yellowjacket, a paper wasp, or whatever. Many simply report that it was a bee and that is how it gets recorded for statistical purposes.

Someone who has had a hypersensitive reaction to a bee sting should take reasonable precautions to avoid getting stung and should be prepared to deal with any emergency that should arise. But most people who are hypersensitive will not know they are until they get that second sting and have a reaction. This causes many people to worry about dying from a second sting. As mentioned above, however, there are very few people who are that sensitive and, as one expert puts it, you probably face more danger of dying in a car wreck on the way to the hospital to be treated for a sting than you face from the sting itself.

If you suspect that you are hypersensitive, a doctor can perform a skin test using a small amount of venom. A negative test will not necessarily rule out development of the allergy at some future time but a positive test will at least provide you with some warning. Someone diagnosed as having a hypersensitivity to bee stings should discuss what measures to take with his or her physician. One suggestion the doctor will probably make is to carry a sting kit, especially when taking part in outdoor activities during the times of year when bees are active. These kits generally include an epinephrine (adrenaline) injector or an inhaler. Adrenaline inhalers often work well in situations of anaphylactic trauma because they get directly to the swelling in the throat that can cause victims to suffocate. Injector kits are easy to use and can be obtained with a doctor's prescription. Follow the directions given by your doctor or those provided with the kit in both cases. Another good idea is to wear a "Medic Alert" bracelet, which indicates that the person wearing it has an insect sting hypersensitivity.

The doctor may also recommend immunotherapy, which involves small injections of the allergen over a period of time to reduce the body's reaction to it. The first shot may contain only a millionth part of the venom with the amounts being slowly increased in following treatments. This can take several months. The bees themselves usually perform this service for their keepers. When someone starts out in beekeeping, he or she will get some nasty stings, especially if the hands are left unprotected. Some beginning beekeepers develop uncomfortable swelling from the fingers to the elbow for a day or two. With each sting, however, the body becomes less sensitive to the venom. Many experienced beekeepers can take dozens of stings from their bees almost without feeling a thing. Many of them deliberately entice bees to sting them in order to maintain their de-sensitized state.

Danger from massive stinging

While most deaths related to insect stings in the United States today are due to allergic reactions, there have also been cases of mass envenomation from multiple stings, and honey bees have almost always been the culprits. One of the first deaths from bee stings to occur in Texas in the period following the arrival of Africanized bees was produced by ordinary European bees. The victim was an elderly man who kept bees on his property. He took 100 stings, far fewer than most healthy, full-grown men would be able to withstand, but his age and general condition probably contributed to his death.

Whether a person attacked by thousands of bees dies from the venom, from a heart attack brought on by the stress, or from falling off a cliff while trying to get away, it is still fair to say the bees were the cause of death. The most important consideration then, should be the avoidance of such an encounter and, secondly, the precautions mentioned above to protect oneself and others in case of an attack. If someone does suffer a massive number of stings, however, there will be a danger of anaphylactic shock, just as there is in the case of allergic reactions. The first thing that should be done, obviously, is to get the victim away from the bees to prevent any further stinging. The next priority should be getting the person to a hospital. If the incident occurs in a remote area, an injection of epinephrine could be administered, especially if there are symptoms of anaphylaxis. First aid procedures that would apply to shock victims in general can also help.

The Africanized bee's venom is almost the same as that of European bees and someone who is sensitive to one will probably react to the other as well. Since they are slightly smaller, each individual Africanized bee carries slightly less venom, but this difference is of trivial importance when massive attacks occur. The body's immune system can be overwhelmed by the introduction of a large amount of venom and there is no antivenin available as yet that can neutralize the poison from Africanized bees.

Even after a person who has suffered massive stings has been treated and appears to be okay, there could be reactions developing to the venom within the body that will not manifest themselves for several days. If someone has taken hundreds of stings, there is a danger of hemolysis, or deterioration of red blood cells, and muscle tissue breakdown which can lead to kidney stress and even kidney failure. The victim should pay close attention to body functions in the days following the stinging incident and consult a physician for a follow up examination.

Body size and general health play an important role in surviving mass attacks. A strong, healthy man can probably survive more than a thousand stings, whereas a small child could be put in danger by a couple of dozen stings. The amount of venom compared to body size determines the danger, just as it does in the case of snake, scorpion, and spider bites. On the other hand, it should be noted, an attack involving only a few bees will be of much less danger to a small child than it would be to an adult over the age of 40, since severe allergic reactions in small children are unlikely. The sad truth is that those of us over the age of 40 no longer have the flexible, well-running machinery of our youth. Our immune system cannot respond as efficiently and our vital bodily functions are not as tolerant of extreme stress. The best thing for a child to do when attacked is to run, the best thing for an older adult to do is to not get attacked in the first place!

Bee Prepared

Many of the measures mentioned above would be difficult to apply in the field under the duress of an emergency situation if you have not prepared yourself ahead of time. Most people taking part in normal outdoor activities will not have to go to any extraordinary lengths to be prepared, although certainly a knowledge of basic emergency procedures is always worthwhile.

People involved in activities that take them to remote areas where feral colonies of bees could be encountered should bring along some of the items mentioned above — a tarp or covering, preferably of a light color, a first aid kit, a bee sting kit, head netting and a spray can of insect repellent containing DEET. Leaders of scout troops, participants in hiking activities, fishing and hunting expeditions, and other people who enjoy trekking into the country-side, especially in areas where Africanized bees have been detected, should be prepared just in case.

Another problem that could arise is the appearance of bees in urban parks, lawns, and other areas where there are flowering plants and potential nesting sites. City maintenance crews and park officials should be especially alert for signs of feral colonies. Special efforts should be made to check areas near school yards. The nat-ural curiosity of children, combined with all the reckless abandon of their play behavior, could put them in danger if a particularly defen-sive colony of bees is in the vicinity. Someone in the school should have responsibility for emergency procedures. Unfortunately, many schools have eliminated their staff nurses because of budget cut-backs and there have been cases of children with severe food aller-gies going into trauma because no one was available in the school who was authorized to administer a shot of epinephrine. A massive attack by bees on a children's playground could be disastrous if advance preparations have not been put in place.

Having discussed all the terrible things that could happen and all the precautions that should be taken, it might be good to close on a more positive note. Justin Schmidt, an expert on insect stings at USDA's Carl Hayden Bee Research Center in Tucson, Arizona, notes that death from honey bee stings currently rank near the bottom of statistical death rate tables. Far more people die of sports injuries, lightning strikes, animal bites, asthma attacks and penicillin allergy than die of any type of insect sting, and less than half of the fatalities in that category come from honey bee stings. In a study of annual death statistics, Schmidt found that motor vehicle accidents kill over 1,000 times more people than do insect stings and that deaths connected to smoking occur 3,000 times more than do deaths related to insect stings! Insects kill far fewer people each year than radon gas, slips and falls, electrical accidents, household poisonings, drowning and starvation. So, while reasonable precautions should be taken, remember that even with the arrival of Africanized honey bees in the southern United States, the risk of serious injury or death from bees will remain low in comparison to other dangers that lurk out there in everyday life.

Summary of Bee Sting Treatment

- Take victim from site of attack and seek shelter from bees.

- Remove stings by scraping them out with fingernail or blade — do not try to remove with fingers; you could squeeze more venom out of sac which is still attached to sting.

- If victim receives more than 15 stings and/or displays unusual reaction, such as large-scale swelling, faintness or difficulty in breathing, seek medical attention as soon as possible.

- Immediate treatment — use cold compresses for swelling, administer oral antihistamines and analgesics.

- If victim shows signs of a systemic reaction from allergy or mass envenomation, a shot of epinephrine would be advisable. This can be obtained with a prescription from a doctor, and its use should be discussed with a doctor in advance of any emergency situation that should arise. The doctor may also recommend a kit containing an adrenaline inhalor, which can be especially effective in relieving respiratory problems caused by swelling of air passages.

■ Severe systemic reactions usually occur within 15 minutes of the stinging and are characterized by the following symptoms:

Skin: Flushing and hives

Respiratory: Upper airway obstruction, laryngeal edema (accumulation of fluid in throat) and bronchial spasm

Abdominal: Bowel spasm, diarrhea

General: Circulatory collapse, shock, hypotension, fainting, loss of consciousness

Women may also have uterine contractions

Additional first aid measures could include the application of a tourniquet if stings are limited to the arms and legs. Release the tourniquet for 30 seconds every three minutes to allow some blood flow. Normal treatment for shock may also help — have the victim lie down and loosen belts, ties or other bindings that could restrict breathing and circulation. Cover with a blanket or jacket. Consult a first aid book or a medical professional for additional suggestions on how to be prepared for a bee sting emergency.

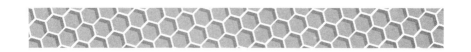

Key "Killer Bee" Dates and Events

1956   Warwick Kerr brings the first queens to Brazil from Africa

1957   Swarms escape from Rio Claro Apiary and begin process of Africanization by mating in the wild and displacing European honey bees

1965   Following reports of mass attacks in Brazil, *Time* magazine runs a story on the phenomenon and uses the term "killer bee"

1976   "Killer bees" reach Venezuela — within a few years, hundreds of deaths are attributed to them

1982   First Africanized bee swarm discovered in Panama

1986   Africanized honey bees enter southern Mexico

1987   Bee regulated zone established in Mexico

1990   Africanized bees discovered near Hidalgo, Texas, in October

1991   Africanized bees attack a man in Brownsville, Texas, the first such attack on U.S. soil

1992   The bee front reaches San Antonio and Corpus Christi

1993   In early July, the invaders reach southern Arizona

1993   On July 15, 82-year-old Lino Lopez, near Harlingen, Texas, becomes the first U.S. fatality from "killer bees"

Management Plans and Contacts in States on the Beeline

THE FOLLOWING STATES HAVE BEEN, OR ARE SOON LIKELY TO BE, invaded by Africanized honey bees. Most have developed a management plan to deal with the problem and more information can be obtained from the offices listed.

ALABAMA

No specific plan yet developed for Africanized bee problem, other than setting some trap lines and monitoring progress of the bees in neighboring states, but basic information on beekeeping and honey production is available from:

Guy W. Karr, Plant Pest Administrator
Alabama Department of Agriculture and Industries
Plant Protection Section
P.O. Box 3336
Montgomery, AL 36109-0336

Telephone: (205) 242-2656
FAX: (205) 240-3135

ARIZONA

Arizona Commission on Agriculture and Horticulture
1688 W. Adams, Room 421
Phoenix, AZ 87007

Telephone: (602) 542-4373
FAX: (602) 542-5420

CALIFORNIA

California Department of Food and Agriculture
1220 N Street, Room 304
Sacramento, CA 95814

Telephone: (916) 445-3588
FAX: (916) 322-5913

In addition, some counties, notably San Diego, have taken an early lead on this issue and have developed their own local programs. Contact the local county Agricultural commissioner.

In San Diego, contact:

Sally Hazzard, Director
Department of Animal Control
5480 Gaines Street
San Diego, CA 92110-2624

Telephone: (619) 531-6041

Other good sources of information are:

California Department of Health Services
714/744 P Street
Sacramento, CA 95814

Publications Office,
Division of Agriculture and Natural Resources
University of California
6701 San Pablo Avenue
Oakland, CA 94608-1239

Telephone: (415) 642-2431

FLORIDA

Florida Department of Agriculture
Division of Plant Industry
1911 SW 34th Street
Gainesville, FL 32608

Telephone: (904) 372-3505
FAX: (904) 374-6801

Florida was the first state to establish an Africanized Bee task force in 1985. USDA is assisting the state in monitoring bait hives at ports and in educating dock workers and ship crews on how to report presence of bees. The state also has close monitoring of apiaries and works closely with the Florida State Beekeepers Association and the 12 local beekeeper associations found in the state.

Information from the Florida State Beekeepers Association may be obtained from the following two people:

John P. Westervelt, President
P.O. Box 630
Umatilla, FL 32784

Telephone: (904) 669-3498

Ralph Russ, (past president)
P.O. Box 398
Lake Hamilton, FL 33851

Telephone: (904) 439-4171

Two good contacts at the University of Florida:

Dr Malcom T Sanford, Extension Entomology
Dr Glenn H Hall, Department of Entomology and Nematology,
Bldg 970, Hull Road
Gainesville, FL 32611-0740

Telephone: (904) 392-1801; Dr Sanford, ext.143, Dr Hall, ext.149

GEORGIA

Georgia Department of Agriculture
Room 300 Capitol Square
Atlanta, GA 30334

Telephone: (404) 656-3689
FAX: (404) 656-9380

Recently developed plan includes an advisory board to coordinate state agencies and to maintain contact with beekeepers. State officials are basing plans on assumption that the Africanized bee will eventually become established throughout the state.

LOUISIANA

Louisiana Department of Agriculture and Forestry
5825 Florida Blvd.
Baton Rouge, LA 70806

Telephone: (504) 922-1234
FAX: (504) 922-1253

MISSISSIPPI

Mississippi Department of Agriculture
Division of Plant Industry, P.O. Box 5027
Mississippi State, MS 39762

Telephone: (601) 325-3390
FAX: (601) 325-8397

NEW MEXICO

New Mexico Department of Agriculture
Bureau of Entomology and Nursery Industries
P.O. Box 30005, Dept. 3BA
Las Cruces, NM 88003-0005

Telephone: (505) 646-2804 or 646-3207
FAX: (505) 646-3303

Governor's Task Force on Africanized Honey Bee is already at work, coordinating activities of several state agencies and county agricultural extension officials. Trap lines being set along Pecos and Rio Grande rivers and in border areas.

TEXAS

Texas A & M University
229 Reed McDonald Building
College Station, TX 77843-2112

Telephone: (409) 845-2895
FAX: (409) 845-2414

Best place to start in getting information in Texas is with the county Agricultural Extension Office or with the local Pest Control Board. Some communities, notably, San Antonio, have implemented educational programs and have literature available. Educational kits developed by the state are also available for schools.

The US Department of Agriculture (USDA) has been involved in the Africanized honey bee issue for more than two decades and has coordinated with state and local agencies in preparing for the arrival of the bees. Beekeepers, farmers, science students, and others interested in USDA research and control programs can contact the following offices:

FOR GENERAL INFORMATION:

USDA Office of Public Affairs
Room 213-A, Admin Bldg.
US Department of Agriculture
14th and Independence Avenue, SW
Washington, DC 20250-1000

Telephone: (202) 720-4623

For more technical information, contact the following laboratories operated by USDA's Agricultural Research Service (ARS):

USDA-ARS Bee Research Laboratory
Beltsville, MD 20705

Telephone: (301) 504-8205

USDA-ARS Honey Bee Breeding, Genetics, and Physiology
  Research Laboratory
1157 Ben Hur Road
Baton Rouge, LA 70820

Telephone: (504) 766-6064

USDA-ARS Honey Bee Laboratory
P.O. Box 267, Weslaco, TX 78596

Telephone: (210) 969-2511

USDA-ARS Carl Hayden Bee Research Center
2000 East Allen Road
Tucson, AZ 85719

Telephone: (602) 670-6709

Journals and magazines about bees and beekeeping:

American Bee Journal
Hamilton, IL 62341

Monthly publication with practical information for beekeepers. Lots of homey articles by and for people involved in beekeeping. Even includes some good recipes utilizing honey from time to time. Often features reports on latest research.

Bee Culture
P.O. Box 706, Medina, OH 44258-0706

How to do it articles, plus research and industry reports. Cornell's Roger Morse, one of the best when it comes to describing beekeeping techniques, is a frequent contributor. Regular reports on honey prices and industry happenings.

The Speedy Bee
P.O. Box 998, Jesup, GA 31545

More oriented to government policies related to beekeeping; also contains some articles on management techniques and research.

International Bee Research Association
18 North Road, Cardiff CF1 3DY,
United Kingdom (England)

Information from around the world on bees, much of it technical in nature, published in three English language journals: *Apicultural Abstracts*, *Bee World*, and *Journal of Apicultural Research*, which is edited by USDA/ARS' Thomas Rinderer.

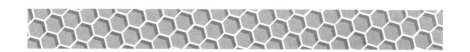

Suggested Books for Further Reading

HERE ARE A FEW BOOKS THAT YOU CAN EITHER CHECK OUT FROM YOUR local library or order through your bookstore if you would like to learn more about Africanized honey bees, honey bees in general, and beekeeping. There are many other works available, but these will give you a good start.

Gould, James and Gould, Carol Grant, *The Honey Bee*. New York: Scientific American Library, 1988.

Wonderful text, illustrations and photos. Almost everything you would ever want to know about honey bees and their behavior.

Graham, Joe, ed., *The Hive and the Honey Bee*. Hamilton, Illinois: Dadant and Sons, 1992.

Collection of chapters dealing with various aspects of bees and beekeeping. Includes a detailed analysis of bee sting venom and reactions to stings by USDA's Justin Schmidt.

Hubbell, Sue, *A Book of Bees*. New York: Ballantine Books, 1988.

A very readable book about the bucolic country life of a beekeeper in Missouri who truly loves these little animals. Lots of references to literature and the classics — as the author puts it, "beekeeping is farming for intellectuals." She dedicated the book to *Apis mellifera*.

Morse, Roger, *The Complete Guide to Beekeeping*. New York: E.P. Dutton, 1986.

A great introduction to the subject by a real master.

Morse, Roger and Hooper, Ted, *The Illustrated Encyclopedia of Beekeeping*, New York: E.P. Dutton, 1985.

A great reference work, with some nice photos as well. Fun to browse through.

Root, A.I et al., Morse, Roger and Flottum, Kim, eds. *ABC and XYZ of Bee Culture*, 40th edition. Medina, Ohio: A.I. Root Co., 1991.

A good general reference on bees and beekeeping.

Roubik, David, *Ecology and Natural History of Tropical Bees*. New York: Cambridge University Press, 1989.

A bit technical for the average lay person, but one of the best sources of information on the tropical stingless bees of the Americas.

Spivak, Marla, Fletcher, David and Breed, Michael, *The "African" Honey Bee*. Boulder, Colorado: Westview Press, 1991.

The technical sourcebook on research of the Africanized honey bees. Very academic and technical for the most part, but a good, basic reference for anyone who wants to approach the subject seriously.

Winston, Mark L., Killer Bees, *The Africanized Honey Bee in the Americas*. Cambridge, Massachusetts: Harvard University Press, 1992.

A good overall look at the subject by one of the researchers who started following the Africanized bees through South America in the 1970's. Although there are some technical discussions, it is written for the average reader.

Whynott, Douglas, *Following the Bloom; Across America with the Migratory Beekeepers*. Harrisburg, Pennsylvania: Stackpole Books, 1991.

A close look at the life of the migratory "entomological cowboys," who truck their colonies north and south to pollinate the nation's agricultural crops. This is a narrative book that tells stories, explores the character of individual beekeepers, and, along the way, provides a great deal of useful information about honey bees.

Index

144